BIBLE 100
Teacher's Guide Part 2

MW00745632

Author:

Alpha Omega Publications

Editor:

Alan Christopherson, M.S.

Media Credits:

Alpha Omega
PUBLICATIONS

**804 N. 2nd Ave. E.
Rock Rapids, IA 51246-1759**

BIBLE 100

LIFEPAC® Overview

BIBLE SCOPE & SEQUENCE

	Grade 1	Grade 2	Grade 3
UNIT 1	**GOD CREATED ALL THINGS** • God created day and night • God created land and sea • God created plants and animals • God created people	**WHO AM I?** • God made us • God loves me • God helps me • God helped Daniel	**WHY AM I HERE?** • I love and obey God • I praise God • I worship God • I serve God
UNIT 2	**GOD LOVES HIS CHILDREN** • God cared for Shadrach, Meshach, and Abednego • God cared for Joash and Esther • God cares for His Children • God's children love Him	**THE STORY OF MOSES** • The early life of Moses • Life in Midian • Moses returns to Egypt • Life in the desert	**THE LIFE OF JESUS** • Mary and Joseph • Jesus in the Temple • Jesus teaches and saves • Jesus dies and lives again
UNIT 3	**WE CAN PRAY** • We can ask and thank God • We can pray God's special prayer • God listens to us • We listen to God	**GOD AND YOU** • God is great • God keeps his promises • You should obey God • God rewards his people	**GOD'S PLAN FOR JOSEPH** • The dream of Joseph • Joseph and his brothers • Joseph in Egypt • God watched over Joseph
UNIT 4	**GOD WANTS YOU TO BE GOOD** • Jesus says love God • God says to love others • You show your love • God says to love yourself	**HOW THE BIBLE CAME TO US** • Moses and the Prophets • David and Solomon • The Apostles and Paul • Bible translators	**YOU CAN USE THE BIBLE** • The books of the Bible • How to read and study the Bible • How to find verses • How to memorize verses
UNIT 5	**OLD TESTAMENT STORIES** • Joseph, Elijah, Jonathan, and David • Miriam and Deborah • A rich woman and her son • Ishmael and Mephibosheth	**DAVID'S SLING** • David with the sheep • David and the prophet • David and Saul • David and the giant	**GOD CARES FOR HIS PEOPLE** • God's love for people • God guides people • God protects people • God blesses people
UNIT 6	**GOD'S PROMISE** • God's Old Testament promises • God's promises kept • The birth of the Promised One • The life of the Promised One	**GOD IS EVERYWHERE** • Understanding the beginning • Understanding God • The creation • God's will	**THE BIBLE IS GOD'S WORD** • The writers of God's Word • God's Word is preserved • God's Word changes lives • Promises of God's Word
UNIT 7	**JESUS, OUR SAVIOUR** • Jesus taught the people • Jesus healed the people • Jesus saves the people • Jesus will come again	**THE STORY OF JOSEPH** • Joseph as a boy at home • The worship of Joseph • Joseph in Egypt • Joseph and the famine	**ARCHAEOLOGY AND THE BIBLE** • The search for treasure • Clues from old stories • Explaining the puzzles • Joining the search
UNIT 8	**GOD CALLS MISSIONARIES** • The woman at the well • Stephen and Paul • Missionaries today • God calls missionaries	**GOD AND THE FAMILY** • The first family • Abraham's family • Happy families • God's promise to children	**THE NEED FOR FRIENDS** • We need love • We need friendship • God commands our love • Love for others
UNIT 9	**NEW TESTAMENT STORIES** • Lazarus, Thomas, Stephen • Mary, Anna, Lydia • Children in the New Testament • Jesus and the Children	**GOD MADE THE NATIONS** • The people of Babel • God's judgment at Babel • The new nation • Our big world	**GOD'S PEOPLE HELP OTHERS** • All people are created by God • God loves me • God's love to others • God is my Father
UNIT 10	**GOD GAVE YOU MANY GIFTS** • God created all things • God loves His children • God gave us His Word • God gave us His Son	**GOD, HIS WORD, AND YOU** • God as our Father • The Word of God • Life with God • Belonging to God	**GOD'S WORD, JESUS, AND YOU** • God speaks to Man • Writers of the Word • Jesus and the Word • God's family

BIBLE SCOPE & SEQUENCE

Grade 4	Grade 5	Grade 6	
HOW CAN I LIVE FOR GOD? • Peter found Jesus • Peter Fished for Men • To be born into God's family • To be fruitful through the Spirit	**HOW OTHERS LIVED FOR GOD** • Fellow-laborers with God • Abraham, a man of faith • Servants of God • Co-workers with God	**FROM CREATION TO MOSES** • Creation • The Flood • Abraham and his descendants • Moses and the Law	UNIT 1
GOD'S KNOWLEDGE • Knowledge to create • Learning God's knowledge • The benefits of God's knowledge • Using God's knowledge	**ANGELS** • Characteristics of Angels • Kinds of Angels • The ministry of Angels • Angels in the life of Jesus	**FROM JOSHUA TO SAMUEL** • Conquest and division of the land • The death of Joshua • The Judges of Israel • Ruth, Naomi, and Boaz	UNIT 2
SAUL BEGINS TO LIVE FOR GOD • Saul persecutes the Christians • God changes Saul • Saul preaches about Jesus • Paul belongs to Christ	**THE PRESENCE OF GOD** • Everywhere as God • Everywhere as a person • In the lives of people • In my life	**THE KINGDOM OF ISRAEL** • Samuel and Saul • The reign of David • The reign of Solomon • The books of poetry	UNIT 3
THE BIBLE AND ME • Reading and learning the Bible • Thinking about the Bible • Memorizing the Bible • Living the Bible way	**BIBLE METHODS AND STRUCTURE** • One book with many parts • Books of history • Books of poetry and prophecy • Books of the New Testament	**THE DIVIDED KINGDOM** • From Jeroboam to Captivity • Prophets of Judah and Israel • From Hezekiah to Captivity • Prophets of remaining kingdom	UNIT 4
GOD CARES FOR US • The Twenty-third Psalm • Jesus and the sheep • David as a shepherd • Daniel as a helper	**THE CHRISTIAN IN THE WORLD** • Instruction and correction • Learning correct behavior • Relationships at school • Relationships in the world	**CAPTIVITY AND RESTORATION** • The prophets of the captivity • The returns from exile • The prophets of the Restoration • Creation to Restoration	UNIT 5
HOW CAN I KNOW GOD EXISTS • God's plan for the Jews • A Jewish Savior • Man searches for God • Man needs God	**PROVING WHAT WE BELIEVE** • The Bible is God's Word • Evidence from the Bible • Evidence from history and science • Knowing that Christ arose	**THE LIFE OF JESUS** • Birth and background • The first years of ministry • The latter years of ministry • The death and Resurrection	UNIT 6
OLD TESTAMENT GEOGRAPHY • Bible Geography • Description of the Land • Abram's Nomadic Life • Abraham's Descendants	**MISSIONARY JOURNEYS OF PAUL** • Paul's background • Paul's missionary journeys • The Jerusalem Council • Paul's last years	**THE FOLLOWERS OF JESUS** • The disciples of Jesus • The friends of Jesus • Miracles of Jesus • The message of Jesus	UNIT 7
GOD-GIVEN WORTH • Who Am I? • God is my Creator • God is my Father • Knowing God's Love	**GOD CREATED MAN FOR ETERNITY** • Preparing for eternity • Christ is our Judge • The judgment of the Christian • The judgment of the unsaved	**THE APOSTLE PAUL** • Paul's background and conversion • Paul's missionary journeys • Paul's letters to churches • Paul's letters to people	UNIT 8
WITNESSING FOR JESUS • Loving God and Others • Following Jesus • Knowing who Jesus is • Following Paul's Example	**AUTHORITY AND LAW** • God is the source of law • The model of law • The authority of the family • Our authority of government	**HEBREWS AND GENERAL EPISTLES** • The book of Hebrews • James and 1st and 2nd Peter • The three Johns • The book of Jude	UNIT 9
GOD'S WAY IS PERFECT • Seeking Knowledge • Science & Geography • Living God's Way • Loving God's Way	**ANGELS, THE BIBLE, LIVING FOR GOD** • Presence of God and Angels • Understanding the Bible • Areas of service • The order of authority	**REVELATION AND REVIEW** • The Lord Jesus in Revelation • End-time events • Old Testament review • New Testament review	UNIT 10

BIBLE SCOPE & SEQUENCE

	Grade 7	Grade 8	Grade 9
UNIT 1	**WORSHIP** • The nature of worship • Old Testament worship • New Testament worship • True worship	**PRAYER** • Organization of the Lord's Prayer • Purpose of the Lord's Prayer • History of prayer • Practical uses of prayer	**THE NEW TESTAMENT** • Inter-Testamental period • Pharisees and Sadducees • New Testament themes • New Testament events
UNIT 2	**MANKIND** • The origin of man • The fall of man • The re-creation of man • The mission of man	**SIN AND SALVATION** • The nature of sin • The need for salvation • How to receive salvation • The results of salvation	**THE GOSPELS** • Matthew • Mark • Luke • John
UNIT 3	**THE ATTRIBUTES OF GOD** • God's nature of love • God's expression of love • The mercy of God • The grace of God	**ATTRIBUTES OF GOD** • God's justice • God's immutability • God's eternal nature • God's love	**THE ACTS OF THE APOSTLES** • The writer • The purpose • Pentecost • Missions
UNIT 4	**FULFILLED PROPHECIES OF CHRIST** • Method of the First Advent • Purpose of the First Advent • Offices of the Messiah foretold • Offices of the Messiah fulfilled	**EARLY CHURCH LEADERS** • The early church • The church of the Middle Ages • The Renaissance • The Reformation	**THE PAULINE EPISTLES** • Paul as a person • The early epistles • Prison epistles • The later epistles
UNIT 5	**NEW LIFE IN CHRIST** • Life before and after Christ • Growing in Christ • Life in the Spirit • The life of grace	**EARLY CHURCH HISTORY** • The Roman Empire • The background of the Jews • The ministry of Jesus • The Jerusalem church	**GENERAL EPISTLES** • James • First and Second Peter • First, Second, and Third John • Hebrews and Jude
UNIT 6	**THE PSALMS** • The history of the Psalms • Types and uses of the Psalms • Hebrew poetry • Study of Psalm 100	**THE EARLY CHURCHES** • The church at Antioch • The missionary journeys • The Jerusalem Conference • New Testament churches	**THE REVELATION OF JESUS CHRIST** • The seven churches • The seven seals and trumpets • The seven signs and plagues • The seven judgments and wonders
UNIT 7	**THE LIFE OF CHRIST: PART ONE** • Early life of Christ • Beginning of Christ's ministry • The early Judean ministry • The early Galilean ministry	**THE BOOK OF PROVERBS** • Literary forms and outline • Objectives and purposes • Influence on the New Testament • Key themes	**JOB AND SUFFERING** • The scenes of Job • Attitudes toward suffering • Christ's suffering on Earth • The victory of Christ's suffering
UNIT 8	**THE LIFE OF CHRIST: PART TWO** • The public ministry in Galilee • The private ministry in Galilee • The Judean ministry • The Perean ministry	**TODAY'S PROBLEMS** • Guidance for behavior • Characteristics of friendship • Studying effectively • Finding God's will	**HOW TO SHARE CHRIST** • Personal evangelism • Outreach to others • Personal and family missions • Assisting a missionary
UNIT 9	**THE LIFE OF CHRIST: PART THREE** • Jesus's final ministry • Jesus's sufferings and crucifixion • Jesus's resurrection and ascension	**UNDERSTANDING PARENTS** • Human parents • Biblical parents • Children's responsibility • Parents and children as a team	**GOD'S WILL FOR MY LIFE** • The desire of the heart • The Word and work of God • The importance of goals • The use of talents
UNIT 10	**IN SUMMARY** • God and His plan • Man's history • Jesus Christ fulfills God's plan • Man's response to God	**WALKING WITH GOD** • Prayer and salvation • The attributes of God • The early church leaders • Christian living	**THE WALK WITH CHRIST** • Background of the New Testament • The Epistles and Revelation • The importance of suffering • God's will for my life

BIBLE SCOPE & SEQUENCE

Grade 10	Grade 11	Grade 12	
CREATION TO ABRAHAM • The six days of creation • The fall of man • Noah and his descendants • Nations of the earth	**THE FAITHFULNESS OF GOD** • Affirmation of God's faithfulness • Nature of God's faithfulness • Manifestations of God's faithfulness • Implications of God's faithfulness	**KNOWING YOURSELF** • Your creation by God • Interacting with others • A child and servant of God • Your personal skills	UNIT 1
ABRAHAM TO MOSES • Abraham's call and promise • The covenant with Isaac • The life of Jacob • Joseph and his family	**ROMANS: PART ONE** • The Roman Empire and Church • The book of Romans • Paul's message to the Romans • Sin and salvation in Romans	**CHRISTIAN MINISTRIES** • Christian ministry defined • Church related ministries • Other ministries • A ministry as a career	UNIT 2
EXODUS AND WANDERINGS • The journey to Sinai • The giving of the Law • Numbering the people • The book of Deuteronomy	**ROMANS: PART TWO** • The chosen of God • Service and submission • From sin to salvation • The victory of salvation	**CHOOSING A CHRISTIAN MINISTRY** • Where to look for a ministry • What to look for in a ministry • How to look for a ministry • Choosing a ministry for a career	UNIT 3
ISRAEL IN CANAAN • Preparing for battle • The fight for the land • Dividing the land • The death of Joshua	**THE DOCTRINE OF JESUS CHRIST** • Identity and incarnation of Christ • The individuality of Christ • Christ's work on the Cross • Christ's work after the Cross	**GODHEAD** • Old Testament view • New Testament view • Historical Perspectives • Faith and man's relationship	UNIT 4
THE JUDGES AND SPIRITUAL DECLINE • Background of Judges • History of the Judges • Examples of spiritual decay • Ruth and redemption	**THE NATION OF ISRAEL** • The covenant with Abraham • Israel as a nation • Old Testament archaeology • New Testament archaeology	**ATTRIBUTES OF GOD** • The Holiness of God • The Goodness of God • Holiness and the believer • Goodness and the Creation	UNIT 5
THE KINGDOM • Samuel and Saul • David • Solomon • Hebrew poetry	**HISTORY OF THE CANON** • Revelation and inspiration • Illumination and interpretation • Authority of the Bible • Formation of the Bible	**THE EPISTLES OF JAMES** • James the man • The message of James • John the man • The message of John's epistles	UNIT 6
THE DIVIDED KINGDOM • Jeroboam to Ahab • Ahab to Jehu • Jehu to Assyrian captivity • Prophets of the period	**FRIENDSHIP, DATING, AND MARRIAGE** • Meaning and role of friendship • Perspectives of dating • Principles of relationships • The structure of marriage	**DANIEL** • A man of conviction • An interpreter of dreams • A watchman in prayer • A man of visions	UNIT 7
THE REMAINING KINGDOM • The time of Hezekiah • Manasseh to Josiah • Jehoahaz to the exile • Prophets of the period	**THE PURSUIT OF HAPPINESS** • Solomon's succession • Solomon's prosperity • Solomon's fall • Solomon's reflection	**COMPARATIVE RELIGIONS** • Elements of Christianity • The validity of Christian faith • World religions • The occult	UNIT 8
THE CAPTIVITY • Prophets of the period • Jeremiah • Ezekiel • Daniel	**ANSWERS FOR AGNOSTICS** • Integrity of the Bible • Doctrines of the Bible • Interpretation of the Bible • Application of the Bible	**WISDOM FOR TODAY'S YOUTH** • Life and character of David • Life and riches of Solomon • Psalms and Proverbs • The Bible and literature	UNIT 9
THE RESTORATION • First return from exile • The Jews preserved • Second return from exile • Haggai, Zechariah, and Malachi	**GOD, HIS WORD, AND THE CHRISTIAN** • The uniqueness of the Bible • History of Israel • God revealed in the Bible • Principles for living	**PRACTICAL CHRISTIAN LIVING** • Christian fundamentals • Growing in Christian maturity • A ministry for Christ • A testimony for Christ	UNIT 10

STRUCTURE OF THE LIFEPAC CURRICULUM

The LIFEPAC curriculum is conveniently structured to provide one teacher's guide containing teacher support material with answer keys and ten student worktexts for each subject at grade levels two through twelve. The worktext format of the LIFEPACs allows the student to read the textual information and complete workbook activities all in the same booklet. The easy-to-follow LIFEPAC numbering system lists the grade as the first number(s) and the last two digits as the number of the series. For example, the Language Arts LIFEPAC at the 6th grade level, 5th book in the series would be LAN0605.

Each LIFEPAC is divided into 3 to 5 sections and begins with an introduction or overview of the booklet as well as a series of specific learning objectives to give a purpose to the study of the LIFEPAC. The introduction and objectives are followed by a vocabulary section which may be found at the beginning of each section at the lower levels or in the glossary at the high school level. Vocabulary words are used to develop word recognition and should not be confused with the spelling words introduced later in the LIFEPAC. The student should learn all vocabulary words before working the LIFEPAC sections to improve comprehension, retention, and reading skills.

Each activity or written assignment in grades 2 through 12 has a number for easy identification, such as 1.1. The first number corresponds to the LIFEPAC section and the number to the right of the decimal is the number of the activity.

Teacher checkpoints, which are essential to maintain quality learning, are found at various locations throughout the LIFEPAC. The teacher should check 1) neatness of work and penmanship, 2) quality of understanding (tested with a short oral quiz), 3) thoroughness of answers (complete sentences and paragraphs, correct spelling, etc.), 4) completion of activities (no blank spaces), and 5) accuracy of answers as compared to the answer key (all answers correct).

The self test questions in grades 2 through 12 are also number coded for easy reference. For example, 2.015 means that this is the 15th question in the self test of Section 2. The first number corresponds to the LIFEPAC section, the zero indicates that it is a self test question, and the number to the right of the zero the question number.

The LIFEPAC test is packaged at the centerfold of each LIFEPAC. It should be removed and put aside before giving the booklet to the student for study.

Answer and test keys in grades 2 through 12 have the same numbering system as the LIFEPACs. The student may be given access to the answer keys (not the test keys) under teacher supervision so that he can score his own work.

A thorough study of the LIFEPAC Overview by the teacher before instruction begins is essential to the success of the student. The teacher should become familiar with expected skill mastery and understand how these grade-level skills fit into the overall skill development of the curriculum. The teacher should also preview the objectives that appear at the beginning of each LIFEPAC for additional preparation and planning.

TEST SCORING AND GRADING

Answer keys and test keys give examples of correct answers. They convey the idea, but the student may use many ways to express a correct answer. The teacher should check for the essence of the answer, not for the exact wording. Many questions are high level and require thinking and creativity on the part of the student. Each answer should be scored based on whether or not the main idea written by the student matches the model example. "Any Order" or "Either Order" in a key indicates that no particular order is necessary to be correct.

Most self tests and LIFEPAC tests at the lower elementary levels are scored at 1 point per answer; however, the upper levels may have a point system awarding 2 to 5 points for various answers or questions. Further, the total test points will vary; they may not always equal 100 points. They may be 78, 85, 100, 105, etc.

Example 1

Example 2

A score box similar to ex. 1 above is located at the end of each self test and on the front of the LIFEPAC test. The bottom score, 72, represents the total number of points possible on the test. The upper score, 58, represents the number of points your student will need to receive an 80% or passing grade. If you wish to establish the exact percentage that your student has achieved, find the total points of his correct answers and divide it by the bottom number (in this case 72). For example, if your student has a point total of 65, divide 65 by 72 for a grade of 90%. Referring to ex. 2, on a test with a total of 105 possible points, the student would have to receive a minimum of 84 correct points for an 80% or passing grade. If your student has received 93 points, simply divide the 93 by 105 for a percentage grade of 89%. Students who receive a score below 80% should review the LIFEPAC and retest using the appropriate Alternate Test found in the Teacher's Guide.

The following is a guideline to assign letter grades for completed LIFEPACs based on a maximum total score of 100 points.

Example:

LIFEPAC Test	=	60% of the Total Score (or percent grade)
Self Test	=	25% of the Total Score (average percent of self tests)
Reports	=	10% or 10* points per LIFEPAC
Oral Work	=	5% or 5* points per LIFEPAC

*Determined by the teacher's subjective evaluation of the student's daily work.

Example:

LIFEPAC Test Score	=	92%	92 × .60	=	55 points
Self Test Average	=	90%	90 × .25	=	23 points
Reports				=	8 points
Oral Work				=	4 points

TOTAL POINTS	=	90 points

Grade Scale based on point system:

100 – 94	=	A
93 – 86	=	B
85 – 77	=	C
76 – 70	=	D
Below 70	=	F

TEACHER HINTS AND STUDYING TECHNIQUES

LIFEPAC activities are written to check the level of understanding of the preceding text. The student may look back to the text as necessary to complete these activities; however, a student should never attempt to do the activities without reading (studying) the text first. Self tests and LIFEPAC tests are never open book tests.

Language arts activities (skill integration) often appear within other subject curriculum. The purpose is to give the student an opportunity to test his skill mastery outside of the context in which it was presented.

Writing complete answers (paragraphs) to some questions is an integral part of the LIFEPAC curriculum in all subjects. This builds communication and organization skills, increases understanding and retention of ideas, and helps enforce good penmanship. Complete sentences should be encouraged for this type of activity. Obviously, single words or phrases do not meet the intent of the activity, since multiple lines are given for the response.

Review is essential to student success. Time invested in review where review is suggested will be time saved in correcting errors later. Self tests, unlike the section activities, are closed book. This procedure helps to identify weaknesses before they become too great to overcome. Certain objectives from self tests are cumulative and test previous sections; therefore, good preparation for a self test must include all material studied up to that testing point.

The following procedure checklist has been found to be successful in developing good study habits in the LIFEPAC curriculum.

1. Read the introduction and Table of Contents.
2. Read the objectives.
3. Recite and study the entire vocabulary (glossary) list.
4. Study each section as follows:
   a. Read the introduction and study the section objectives.
   b. Read all the text for the entire section, but answer none of the activities.
   c. Return to the beginning of the section and memorize each vocabulary word and definition.
   d. Reread the section, complete the activities, check the answers with the answer key, correct all errors, and have the teacher check.
   e. Read the self test but do not answer the questions.
   f. Go to the beginning of the first section and reread the text and answers to the activities up to the self test you have not yet done.
   g. Answer the questions to the self test without looking back.
   h. Have the self test checked by the teacher.
   i. Correct the self test and have the teacher check the corrections.
   j. Repeat steps a–i for each section.
5. Use the **SQ3R** method to prepare for the LIFEPAC test.
   > **S**can the whole LIFEPAC.
   > **Q**uestion yourself on the objectives.
   > **R**ead the whole LIFEPAC again.
   > **R**ecite through an oral examination.
   > **R**eview weak areas.
6. Take the LIFEPAC test as a closed book test.
7. LIFEPAC tests are administered and scored under direct teacher supervision. Students who receive scores below 80% should review the LIFEPAC using the **SQ3R** study method and take the Alternate Test located in the Teacher's Guide. The final test grade may be the grade on the Alternate Test or an average of the grades from the original LIFEPAC test and the Alternate Test.

GOAL SETTING AND SCHEDULES

Each school must develop its own schedule, because no single set of procedures will fit every situation. The following is an example of a daily schedule that includes the five LIFEPAC subjects as well as time slotted for special activities.

Possible Daily Schedule

8:15 – 8:25	Pledges, prayer, songs, devotions, etc.
8:25 – 9:10	Bible
9:10 – 9:55	Language Arts
9:55 – 10:15	Recess (juice break)
10:15 – 11:00	Math
11:00 – 11:45	History & Geography
11:45 – 12:30	Lunch, recess, quiet time
12:30 – 1:15	Science
1:15 –	Drill, remedial work, enrichment*

***Enrichment:** Computer time, physical education, field trips, fun reading, games and puzzles, family business, hobbies, resource persons, guests, crafts, creative work, electives, music appreciation, projects.*

Basically, two factors need to be considered when assigning work to a student in the LIFEPAC curriculum.

The first is time. An average of 45 minutes should be devoted to each subject, each day. Remember, this is only an average. Because of extenuating circumstances a student may spend only 15 minutes on a subject one day and the next day spend 90 minutes on the same subject.

The second factor is the number of pages to be worked in each subject. A single LIFEPAC is designed to take 3 to 4 weeks to complete. Allowing about 3 to 4 days for LIFEPAC introduction, review, and tests, the student has approximately 15 days to complete the LIFEPAC pages. Simply take the number of pages in the LIFEPAC, divide it by 15 and you will have the number of pages that must be completed on a daily basis to keep the student on schedule. For example, a LIFEPAC containing 45 pages will require 3 completed pages per day. Again, this is only an average. While working a 45-page LIFEPAC, the student may complete only 1 page the first day if the text has a lot of activities or reports, but go on to complete 5 pages the next day.

Long-range planning requires some organization. Because the traditional school year originates in the early fall of one year and continues to late spring of the following year, a calendar should be devised that covers this period of time. Approximate beginning and completion dates can be noted on the calendar as well as special occasions such as holidays, vacations and birthdays. Since each LIFEPAC takes 3 to 4 weeks or eighteen days to complete, it should take about 180 school days to finish a set of ten LIFEPACs. Starting at the beginning school date, mark off eighteen school days on the calendar and that will become the targeted completion date for the first LIFEPAC. Continue marking the calendar until you have established dates for the remaining nine LIFEPACs making adjustments for previously noted holidays and vacations. If all five subjects are being used, the ten established target dates should be the same for the LIFEPACs in each subject.

TEACHING SUPPLEMENTS

The sample weekly lesson plan and student grading sheet forms are included in this section as teacher support materials and may be duplicated at the convenience of the teacher.

The student grading sheet is provided for those who desire to follow the suggested guidelines for assignment of letter grades as previously discussed. The student's self test scores should be posted as percentage grades. When the LIFEPAC is completed, the teacher should average the self test grades, multiply the average by .25, and post the points in the box marked self test points. The LIFEPAC percentage grade should be multiplied by .60 and posted. Next, the teacher should award and post points for written reports and oral work. A report may be any type of written work assigned to the student whether it is a LIFEPAC or additional learning activity. Oral work includes the student's ability to respond orally to questions which may or may not be related to LIFEPAC activities or any type of oral report assigned by the teacher. The points may then be totaled and a final grade entered along with the date that the LIFEPAC was completed.

The Student Record Book which was specifically designed for use with the Alpha Omega curriculum provides space to record weekly progress for one student over a nine-week period as well as a place to post self test and LIFEPAC scores. The Student Record Books are available through the current Alpha Omega catalog; however, unlike the enclosed forms, these books are not for duplication and should be purchased in sets of four to cover a full academic year.

WEEKLY LESSON PLANNER

Week of:

	Subject	Subject	Subject	Subject
Monday				
Tuesday	Subject	Subject	Subject	Subject
Wednesday	Subject	Subject	Subject	Subject
Thursday	Subject	Subject	Subject	Subject
Friday	Subject	Subject	Subject	Subject

WEEKLY LESSON PLANNER

Week of:

	Subject	Subject	Subject	Subject
Monday				
Tuesday	Subject	Subject	Subject	Subject
Wednesday	Subject	Subject	Subject	Subject
Thursday	Subject	Subject	Subject	Subject
Friday	Subject	Subject	Subject	Subject

Student Name _____   Year _____

Bible

LP	Self Test Scores by Sections					Self Test Points	LIFEPAC Test	Oral Points	Report Points	Final Grade	Date
	1	2	3	4	5						
01											
02											
03											
04											
05											
06											
07											
08											
09											
10											

History & Geography

LP	Self Test Scores by Sections					Self Test Points	LIFEPAC Test	Oral Points	Report Points	Final Grade	Date
	1	2	3	4	5						
01											
02											
03											
04											
05											
06											
07											
08											
09											
10											

Language Arts

LP	Self Test Scores by Sections					Self Test Points	LIFEPAC Test	Oral Points	Report Points	Final Grade	Date
	1	2	3	4	5						
01											
02											
03											
04											
05											
06											
07											
08											
09											
10											

Student Name _____   Year _____

Math

LP	Self Test Scores by Sections					Self Test Points	LIFEPAC Test	Oral Points	Report Points	Final Grade	Date
	1	2	3	4	5						
01											
02											
03											
04											
05											
06											
07											
08											
09											
10											

Science

LP	Self Test Scores by Sections					Self Test Points	LIFEPAC Test	Oral Points	Report Points	Final Grade	Date
	1	2	3	4	5						
01											
02											
03											
04											
05											
06											
07											
08											
09											
10											

Spelling/Electives

LP	Self Test Scores by Sections					Self Test Points	LIFEPAC Test	Oral Points	Report Points	Final Grade	Date
	1	2	3	4	5						
01											
02											
03											
04											
05											
06											
07											
08											
09											
10											

INSTRUCTIONS FOR FIRST GRADE BIBLE

The first grade Teacher's Guides of the LIFEPAC curriculum are designed to provide a step-by step procedure that will help the teacher prepare for and present each lesson effectively. In the early LIFEPACs, the teacher should read the directions and any other sentences to the children. However, as the school year progresses, the student should be encouraged to begin reading and following his own instructional material in preparation for the independent study approach that begins at the second grade level.

This section of the Teacher's Guide includes the following teacher aids:
1) Teacher Instruction Pages
2) Cumulative Word List
3) Cumulative Memory Verse List

The Teacher Instruction Pages list the Concept to be taught as well as Student Objectives and Goals for the Teacher. The Teaching Page contains directions for teaching that page. The Activities section at the end of each lesson is optional and may be used to reinforce or expand the concepts taught.

Materials needed are usually items such as pencils and crayons which are readily available. Additional items that may be required are writing tablets or any lined paper, alphabet cards, color and number charts, and flashcards for vocabulary words.

The Cumulative Word List is made up of words introduced at least once in one of the ten subject LIFEPACs. An asterisk (*) following a word indicates a direction-word that the children will need to know by sight to complete the work independently. Sight words are words that either are needed before their phonetic presentation or do not follow the standard phonetic rules. These words need to be learned through memorization and children should be drilled on them frequently. The drill may be done by use of a chart posted in a prominent place, by word card drills, or by word recognition or meaning games. Some words on the Cumulative Word List are not expected to be part of the student's reading vocabulary but part of his speaking vocabulary for better understanding of subject content.

A Cumulative List of Memory Verses is included in the back of this guide. This can be duplicated and kept for easy reference as the students work on learning the verses.

BIBLE 106

Unit 6: God's Promise to Men

GOD'S PROMISE TO MEN
BIBLE 106

Alpha Omega
PUBLICATIONS

804 N. 2nd Ave. E.
Rock Rapids, IA 51246-1759

Author:
Mary Ellen Quint, Ph.D.

Editor:
Rudolph Moore, Ph.D.

Consulting Editor:
John L. Booth, Th.D.

Revision Editor:
Alan Christopherson, M.S.

Media Credits:
Page 1: © graphic-bee, iStock, Thinkstock; **2:**
© stockakia, iStock, Thinkstock; **3:** © LCOSMO,
iStock, Thinkstock.

|i

PAGE 1: GOD'S PROMISE TO MEN

MATERIALS NEEDED

- pencils

Concept:

Purpose of the LIFEPAC.

Objective:

To introduce all the objectives.

Teacher Goal:

To introduce all the objectives.

Reading Integration:

Main idea

Teaching Page 1:

Read the title. Ask the children how many know what a promise is. Ask them to read the first sentence. Ask if they know what God's promise was. Read the final sentences.

Read the objectives. Remind the children that objectives tell them what they will be able to do when they have completed the LIFEPAC.

Have the children repeat the objectives after you and copy them into their writing tablets.

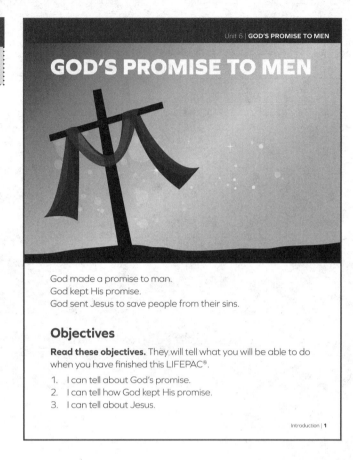

Unit 6 | **GOD'S PROMISE TO MEN**

GOD'S PROMISE TO MEN

God made a promise to man.
God kept His promise.
God sent Jesus to save people from their sins.

Objectives

Read these objectives. They will tell what you will be able to do when you have finished this LIFEPAC®.

1. I can tell about God's promise.
2. I can tell how God kept His promise.
3. I can tell about Jesus.

Introduction | **1**

1.   GOD'S PROMISE

PAGES 2 AND 3: ADAM AND EVE

MATERIALS NEEDED

- pencils
- writing tablet
- construction paper

Concepts:

Man sinned. God promised to save man from sin.

Objective:

I can tell about God's promise.

Teacher Goal:

To teach the children that God loves them and wants them to be saved.

Bible Reference:

Genesis chapter 3

Reading Integration:

Listening, recalling details, main idea, speaking in a group

Vocabulary:

promised, (Adam, Eve, garden, beautiful, disobeyed)
Note: Vocabulary words in parentheses were previously introduced and are being reviewed.

Teaching Pages 2 and 3:

Have a child read the title and first sentence at the top of page 2. Read the second sentence to the children.

Ask if they remember what the Old Testament is. Discuss the illustration of Adam and Eve. Ask the children to recall what they learned about Adam and Eve in Bible 101.

Ask the children to identify the Bible reference (Genesis chapter 3) and remind them what it tells them to look for in the Bible.

Read the remaining text on pages 2 and 3.

Reread the text and the Bible chapter and stop to discuss the concepts.

Ask these questions:

"Who made Adam and Eve?"

"What did God give Adam and Eve?"

"What did Adam and Eve do?"

"What does *disobey* mean?"

"What did God do to Adam and Eve?"

Read the direction or have a child read it. Help the children with the sentences if they need help. Check together.

Discuss the two questions in the discussion box. Ask the children why keeping promises is so important. Stress that promises should not be made lightly. Tell them that they should not make promises that they cannot or will not keep.

Activities:

1. Begin a *God's Promise* scrapbook. Give the children construction paper and help them to write or to cut and paste the words *God's Promise* on the paper. Let them decorate the cover with crayon, material scraps, odds and ends. Put the cover in a folder for safe keeping.

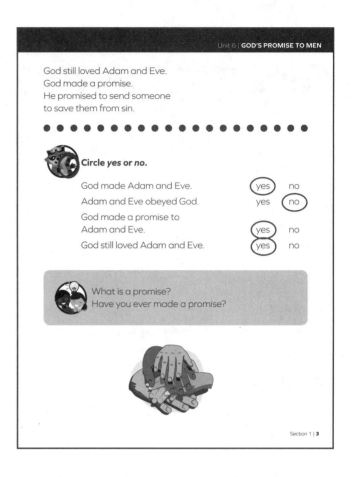

After each lesson in the LIFEPAC, let the children draw, write, or draw and write about the lesson they have completed.

When the LIFEPAC is finished, the scrapbook will be finished. Keep the stories and pictures in a folder until the whole scrapbook is complete.

At the end of the LIFEPAC, help the children to assemble the scrapbook inside the cover. The book may be stapled together or tied with yarn. Putting the scrapbook together will be a good review at the end of the LIFEPAC.

2. Have the children write a paragraph in their writing tablets about promises they have made and kept.

PAGE 4: ABRAHAM

MATERIALS NEEDED

- pencils
- writing tablet
- crayons
- a small amount of sand
- Worksheet 1

Concept:

God's promise to Abraham.

Objective:

I can tell about God's promise.

Teacher Goal:

To teach the children about the promise to Abraham.

Bible Reference:

Genesis 22:15–18

Reading Integration:

Main idea, recalling details

Vocabulary:

Abraham

GOD'S PROMISE TO MEN | Unit 6

Abraham
(Genesis 22:15–18)

Many years later,
God made a promise to Abraham.
God said that someone from Abraham's family would come.
God said that through this person all nations of the earth would be blessed
(Genesis 22:18).

| Abraham

4 | Section 1

Teaching Page 4:

Read the title and the Bible reference to the children. Talk about the promise God made to Abraham. Ask the children if they are able to count all the stars. Show them a small amount (tablespoon) of sand. Ask if they can count the number of grains in the sand. Ask them to imagine how many little grains of sand are in a sandbox or in a whole seashore.

Read the text to the children. Talk about how the nations could be blessed in one person.

Ask the children if they remember any other stories about Abraham.

Activities:

1. Add to *God's Promise* scrapbook.

2. Make an *Abraham* chart. Have the children draw or find pictures about Abraham's life and paste them on the chart. Have them write short paragraphs about Abraham on writing tablet paper. Select the best paragraphs and add them to the chart. Keep the chart and add things later as the children learn more about Abraham.

3. Do Worksheet 1.

    Tell the children that this Worksheet is a riddle.

    Let the children do the page independently if they are able. If not, read each sentence. Tell the children to find the spelling of the name in their LIFEPAC on page 4.

    Check together. Go over each sentence and review what they know about Abraham from Bible 105 and 106.

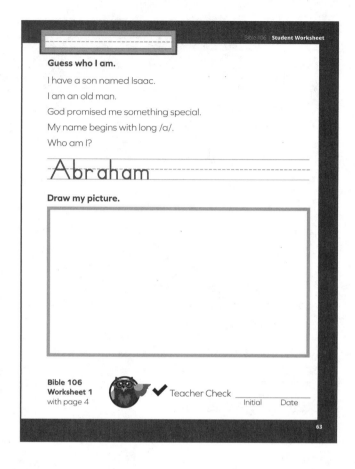

PAGE 5: ACTIVITY PAGE

MATERIALS NEEDED

- pencils
- Worksheet 2

Teaching Page 5:

Read the first direction. Ask a child to read the first sentence and the choices. Let the children write the answer on the line. Have someone read the second sentence and the choices. Let the children write the answer on the line. Check.

Read the second direction. Ask what vowel sound they hear at the beginning of *Abraham* (long /a/). Ask what vowel sound they hear in *nations* (long /a/).

Read the third direction. Talk about other words that have the long /a/ sound. Let them select any two long a words to write on the lines. Help with the spelling.

Activity:

Do Worksheet 2.

Read the directions. Make sure the children know how to follow the puzzle.

Work together if the children are not able to do the page independently.

Check together when they have finished.

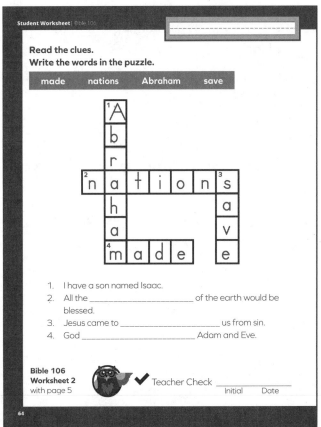

PAGE 6: ISAIAH

MATERIALS NEEDED

• Bible

Concept:

Isaiah tells the people of God's promise.

Objective:

I can tell about God's promise.

Teacher Goal:

To teach the children that God can speak through others.

Bible References:

Isaiah 7:14, 9:6, 11:1–8, 40:1–11, Matthew 1:23

Vocabulary:

Isaiah, (prophet)
Note: Vocabulary words in parentheses were previously introduced and are being reviewed.

Teaching Page 6:

Help children to find the Book of Isaiah in the Bible. Read the title and the Bible references to the children. Remind them how to read and locate each reference.

Read the text to the children. Tell the children that sometimes keeping a promise takes a very long time.

Talk about prophets and their role in God's plan. Explain very simply how God spoke to the people of the Old Testament through special people called prophets.

Help the children to find Isaiah 7:14 in their Bibles.

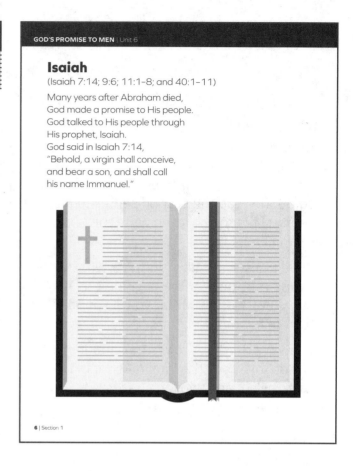

GOD'S PROMISE TO MEN | Unit 6

Isaiah

(Isaiah 7:14; 9:6; 11:1–8; and 40:1–11)

Many years after Abraham died, God made a promise to His people. God talked to His people through His prophet, Isaiah. God said in Isaiah 7:14, "Behold, a virgin shall conceive, and bear a son, and shall call his name Immanuel."

6 | Section 1

Activities:

1. Continue *God's Promise* scrapbook.

2. Read the Bible references to Isaiah. Many may already be familiar to them.

PAGE 7: ACTIVITY PAGE

MATERIALS NEEDED

• pencils
• writing tablet

Teaching Page 7:

Read the memory verse to the children. Remember: A cumulative list of Memory Verses is included. Ask them if it sounds like the quote from Isaiah that they read on page 6. Read Matthew 1:22 and 23 to the children. Tell them that Matthew was talking about Isaiah and reminding the people of Isaiah's words.

Read the directions to the children. Let them complete the page independently. Check together.

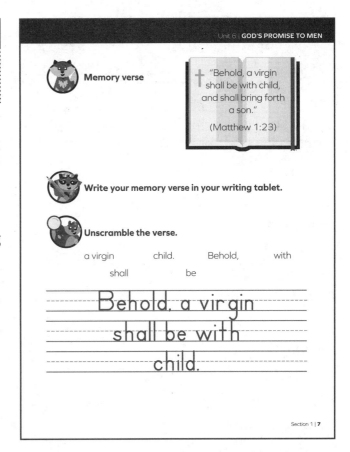

PAGE 8: BETHLEHEM

MATERIALS NEEDED

- Bible

Concept:

God told where the Promised One would be born.

Objective:

I can tell about God's promise.

Teacher Goal:

To teach the children God's careful plan for the birth of the Promised One.

Bible Reference:

Micah 5:2

Reading Integration:

Picture interpretation, listening

Vocabulary:

Bethlehem, Micah

GOD'S PROMISE TO MEN | Unit 6

God told His people many other things about the Promised One. God told these things through Isaiah and through His other prophets.

God's prophet Micah told the people where the Promised One would be born (Micah 5:2):

"Bethlehem … out of thee shall he come forth … that is to be ruler in Israel."

8 | Section 1

Teaching Page 8:

Read the text to the children. Discuss each paragraph. Help the children to find Micah 5:2 in the Bible.

Talk about the care God took to prepare the world for Jesus.

Activities:

1. Add to the scrapbook.

2. Show the children pictures of Bethlehem from a Bible atlas or reference book.

3. Read stories about other people who lived in Bethlehem (recall Bible 105: Ruth and Naomi).

4. Put the word *Bethlehem* on the board. Tell the children to see how many small words they can make from the word. Write them on the board or have the children write them in their writing tablets. *Examples*: Beth, be, the, them, let

5. Make a three dimensional map of the city of Bethlehem. Use a cardboard base and small boxes, twigs, and so on for buildings and plants. You can add to the map in Section 3.

PAGE 9: ACTIVITY PAGE

MATERIALS NEEDED

- pencils
- alphabet chart
- crayons

Teaching Page 9:

Read the directions. If any child is still having difficulty with small letter recognition, encourage him to use his alphabet chart and to work very carefully.

When they have finished, tell the children to trace the name of the city.

The students should prepare for the Self Test. Ask the students to look over and read the Self Test but they should not write the answers to any questions. After looking over the Self Test the students should go to the beginning of the unit and reread the text and review the answers to the activities up to the Self Test.

The students are to complete the Self Test the next school day. This should be done under regular test conditions without allowing the students to look back. A good idea is to clip the pages together before the test.

Unit 6 | **GOD'S PROMISE TO MEN**

Connect the dots in alphabetical order. Trace the letters on the lines. Color the picture.

Bethlehem

Before you take the Self Test, study what you have read and done. The Self Test will check what you remember.

Section 1 | **9**

PAGE 10: SELF TEST 1

MATERIALS NEEDED

• pencils

Concept:

Evaluation.

Objective:

I can tell about God's promise.

Teacher Goal:

To check each child's progress.

Bible References:

Review memory verse and all references.

Reading Integration:

Following written directions, recalling details

Vocabulary:

Review all vocabulary words.

Teaching Page 10:

Review vocabulary and Bible verse before beginning the test.

Read all the directions and sentences if necessary. Let the children finish the test on their own.

Check immediately. Show each child where he has done well and where he needs more work.

Review any concepts missed.

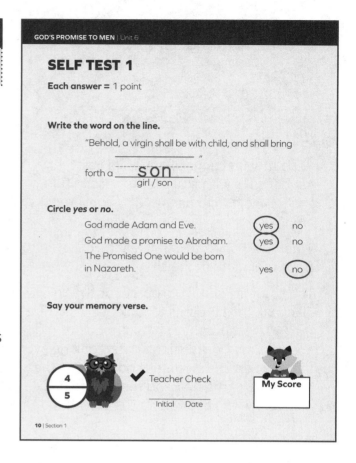

2. GOD'S PROMISE KEPT

PAGE 11

Concept:

God keeps His promises.

Objective:

I can tell how God kept His promise.

Teacher Goal:

To introduce the children to Section 2.

Reading Integration:

Main idea

Vocabulary:

Gabriel, Zacharias, Mary, (Joseph)
Note: Vocabulary words in parentheses were previously introduced and are being reviewed.

Teaching Page 11:

Read the title of the second section.

Read the text. Tell the children that the pictures show the people they will read about in this section (Zacharias, Mary, Joseph, John).

Unit 6 | **GOD'S PROMISE TO MEN**

2. GOD'S PROMISE KEPT

After many years,
God kept His promise.
He sent His angel Gabriel
to Zacharias, Mary, and Joseph.

| Zacharias

| Joseph

| John

| Mary

Secction 2 | **11**

PAGES 12 AND 13: ZACHARIAS

MATERIALS NEEDED

- Bible
- pencils
- crayons
- Worksheet 3

Zacharias
(Luke 1:5–25)

Now God was ready
to keep His promise.
He did something very special.

First, God sent an angel named Gabriel
to talk to His priest, Zacharias.
The angel told Zacharias
that he and his wife Elisabeth
would have a son.

12 | Section 2

Concept:

God's announcement to Zacharias.

Objective:

I can tell how God kept His promise.

Teacher Goal:

To teach the children about God's special preparations for the Promised One.

Bible References:

Luke 1:5–25, 57–66

Reading Integration:

Listening, main idea, picture interpretation

Vocabulary:

angel, Elisabeth, (Zacharias)
Note: Vocabulary words in parentheses were previously introduced and are being reviewed.

Teaching Pages 12 and 13:

Read the title and the first paragraph.

Explain the Bible verses in this section will be taken from the Gospels in the New Testament.

Help the children to find the Gospel of Luke in their Bibles.

Read the text.

Ask the children some questions:

"Who sent an angel?"
"What was the angel's name?"
"How is the picture of the angel different?"
"Why?"
"Who did the angel talk to?"
"What did he tell Zacharias?"
"What name would the son have?"
"What special job would John do when he grew up?"
"Why was Jesus coming?"

Ask the children if they can tell you what name John usually has when they talk about him today. (John the Baptist)

Read the direction and the names. Let the children match. Check together and discuss each character's role.

Read the Bible account and explain more details of the story. (Zacharias's inability to talk, the naming of the baby, etc.)

Activities:

1. Continue scrapbook.

2. Have the children act out Luke 1:5–25, 57–66. Children enjoy acting out these particular stories because they are interested by Zacharias's inability to speak and by the scene of choosing the name.

3. Do Worksheet 3.

   Review words for ordinal numbers first through fourth.

   Read the directions. Let the children do the page independently.

   Check by having the children name the pictures in order and tell the story for each.

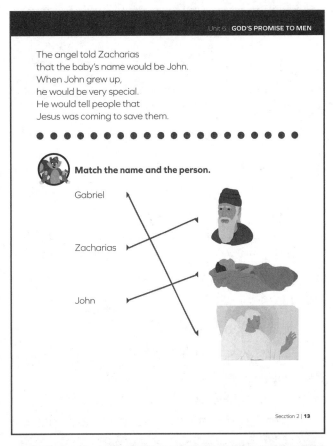

PAGE 14: MARY

MATERIALS NEEDED

- Bible
- writing tablet

Concept:

God chooses a mother for Jesus.

Objective:

I can tell how God kept His promise.

Teacher Goal:

To teach the children about the mother of Jesus.

Bible Reference:

Luke 1:26–38

Reading Integration:

Listening, main idea, retelling the story

Vocabulary:

Nazareth, (angel, Gabriel, Mary)
Note: Vocabulary words in parentheses were previously introduced and are being reviewed.

GOD'S PROMISE TO MEN | Unit 6

Mary
(Luke 1:26–38)

Six months after the angel talked to Zacharias, God sent His angel to the city of Nazareth. The angel Gabriel talked to Mary. He told her that God had picked her to be the mother of Jesus.

14 | Secction 2

Teaching Page 14:

Discuss the illustration. Ask the children why the angel is different.

Have a child read the title.

Read the text. Read it again as the children follow along.

Ask these questions:

"When did the angel come to Mary?"

"Where did Mary live?"

"What was the angel's name?"

"What did the angel tell Mary?"

Read the Bible account and discuss the story more fully.

Activities:

1. Continue scrapbook.

2. After reading the Bible account, especially Luke 1:29 and 30, ask the children to write a paragraph in their writing tablets telling how they would feel if an angel suddenly started talking to them. Discuss the paragraphs when they finish.

3. Have the children act out the story.

PAGE 15: ACTIVITY PAGE

MATERIALS NEEDED

- pencils
- writing tablet
- Bible

Teaching Page 15:

Read the memory verse. Remember: A cumulative list of Memory Verses is included. Have the children repeat it. Have them find it in their Bibles. Ask them who the "He" refers to. (Jesus)

Read the directions. Let the children complete the page independently.

Check together and discuss as a review of the story.

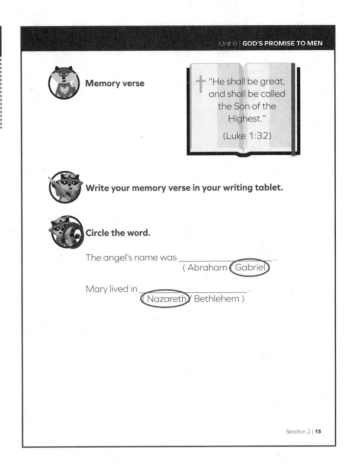

Memory verse

"He shall be great, and shall be called the Son of the Highest."
(Luke 1:32)

Write your memory verse in your writing tablet.

Circle the word.

The angel's name was _____ .
(Abraham Gabriel)

Mary lived in _____
(Nazareth Bethlehem)

Secction 2 | **15**

PAGE 16: JOSEPH

MATERIALS NEEDED

• Bibles
• pencils
• Worksheet 4

GOD'S PROMISE TO MEN | Unit 6

Joseph
(Matthew 1:18–25)

Finally one night, God sent His angel
to a man named Joseph.
Joseph loved Mary.
They were going to be married.
The angel told Joseph that Mary was
going to be the mother of Jesus.
He told Joseph that
Jesus was the Promised One.
Isaiah had talked about the Promised One.
Joseph would be the stepfather of Jesus.

16 | Section 2

Concept:

God chooses a stepfather for Jesus.

Objective:

I can tell how God kept His promise.

Teacher Goal:

To teach the children about Joseph.

Bible Reference:

Matthew 1:18–25

Reading Integration:

Listening, main idea, recalling details

Vocabulary:

stepfather, (Joseph)
Note: Vocabulary words in parentheses were previously introduced and are being reviewed.

Teaching Page 16:

Discuss the illustration. Ask the children what Joseph is doing. (sleeping) Ask how God spoke to Joseph. (through an angel in a dream)

Have a child read the title. Ask the children if they remember any other Joseph. (Joseph in Egypt of the Old Testament)

Read the text. Read it again as the children follow along. Explain what stepfather means. Read the Bible account and discuss in more detail. Have the children find the Bible reference and follow along as you read.

Activities:

1. Continue scrapbook.

2. Do Worksheet 4.

   Instruct the children to color each of the figures.

   Have the children cut them out.

   Help them to paste the stands so that the figures will stand by themselves.

   The children may use these figures by themselves or in small groups to retell and recall the stories. They may want to draw different scenes for the background of each.

   Use these figures for the remainder of the LIFEPAC to reinforce the stories.

3. Have the children act out the story.

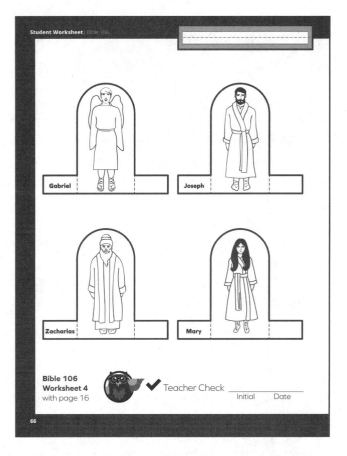

PAGE 17: ACTIVITY PAGE

MATERIALS NEEDED

- crayons
- pencils
- writing tablet

Teaching Page 17:

The reading for this page serves as a review for the section. Discuss the chapter as you read it.

Give each child an opportunity to talk about their pictures. If children have chosen several parts of the story, you may want to call them according to the part of the story their picture represents.

Use this discussion time to review the section for the test.

Activity:

Have the children title three pages of their writing tablets. (first: Zacharias; second: Mary; third: Joseph) Instruct them to write two paragraphs for each title. Allow a day or two to complete. Help them with spelling.

Unit 6 | **GOD'S PROMISE TO MEN**

Listen to your teacher read from Luke 1.
Draw your favorite part of this Bible story.

Before you take the Self Test, study what you have read and done. The Self Test will check what you remember.

Section 2 | **17**

Allow time for the reading of the stories (one per day, perhaps). Check for complete sentences, capital letters, correct punctuation marks at the end, and correctness of details.

The students should prepare for the Self Test. Ask the students to look over and read the Self Test but they should not write the answers to any questions. After looking over the Self Test the students should go to the beginning of the unit and reread the text and review the answers to the activities up to the Self Test.

The students are to complete the Self Test the next school day. This should be done under regular test conditions without allowing the students to look back. A good idea is to clip the pages together before the test.

PAGE 18: SELF TEST 2

MATERIALS NEEDED

• pencils

Concept:

Evaluation.

Objectives:

I can tell about God's promise.

I can tell how God kept His promise.

Teacher Goal:

To check each child's progress.

Bible References:

Review both memory verses and all other references.

Reading Integration:

Following written directions, recalling details

Vocabulary:

Review all vocabulary.

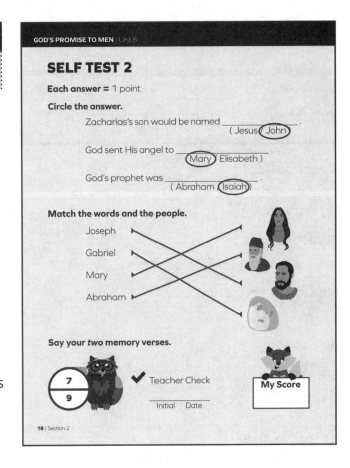

Teaching Page 18:

Review all vocabulary words, especially names, and Bible verses.

Read the directions and the sentences. Let the children complete the page independently. Help with directions and vocabulary, if necessary.

Check immediately. Show each child where he did well and where he needs more work.

Review all concepts missed.

3. GOD'S PROMISED ONE
PAGE 19

Concept:

God sent His only Son to save men from sin.

Objective:

I can tell about Jesus.

Teacher Goal:

To teach the children that Jesus is the Promised Savior.

Bible Reference:

Matthew 1:1–17

Reading Integration:

Main idea, listening

Vocabulary:

(promise, promised, Jesus, Christ)
Note: Vocabulary words in parentheses were previously introduced and are being reviewed.

Teaching Page 19:

Read the title and the text.

Unit 6 | **GOD'S PROMISE TO MEN**

3. GOD'S PROMISED ONE

God kept His promise.
God sent His only Son to Earth.
His Son's name is Jesus.

Jesus was sent
to save His people
from their sins.

Section 3 | **19**

Remind the children of God's promise to Adam and Abraham. Explain very simply Matthew 1:1–17. Tell the children that this genealogy shows them how God's promise that someone from Abraham's family would come. Do not dwell on the complexities of the genealogy. Just tell them that this is like the family tree they made in History & Geography 104.

PAGE 20: A JOURNEY

MATERIALS NEEDED

• Bible

Concept:

The journey to Bethlehem.

Objective:

I can tell about Jesus.

Teacher Goal:

To teach the children how Joseph and Mary went to Bethlehem.

Bible Reference:

Luke 2:1–5

Vocabulary:

journey

Teaching Page 20:

Ask the children what taking a journey means.

Tell them that they will read about a journey that Mary and Joseph took.

Read the first sentence. Ask the children if they remember where the prophet Micah said Jesus would be born. Ask them how Jesus could be born in Bethlehem if Joseph and Mary lived in Nazareth.

Read the remaining text and explain why Mary and Joseph had to go to Bethlehem.

Read the Bible accounts and discuss the story further.

Talk about the illustration. Ask the children why Joseph is carrying a stick. Ask what kind of animal Mary is riding on. Ask what city they see in the distance.

Activities:

1. Continue scrapbook.

2. Act out the story.

3. Use figures (Worksheet 4) to retell the story.

4. Talk about or read stories about journeys.

GOD'S PROMISE TO MEN | Unit 6

A Journey
(Luke 2:1–5)

Mary and Joseph lived in Nazareth. The emperor, Caesar Augustus, ordered a tax just before Jesus was to be born.

Mary and Joseph had to leave their home. They went to Bethlehem to be taxed.

20 | Section 3

PAGE 21: ACTIVITY PAGE

MATERIALS NEEDED

- pencils
- crayons
- simple map of the Land of Israel during the time of the birth of Jesus

Teaching Page 21:

Show the children a simple map of the Land of Israel. Show the children the journey that Mary and Joseph made.

Read the directions. Tell the children to find the way from Nazareth to Bethlehem through the maze. Have them find the way first with their fingers before they use a pencil or crayon.

Activities:

1. If children still have difficulty with mazes, make up simple worksheets with simple mazes for extra practice.

2. Play a journey game. Begin by saying, "I'm going on a journey and I'm taking along a _____ ." (toothbrush, suitcase, book, etc.) The first child then repeats the sentence and item and adds a second item. The next child must repeat the sentence, the first two items, and add a third, and so on. If a child misses an item he is out.

3. Talk about what Mary and Joseph might have taken with them.

Unit 6 | **GOD'S PROMISE TO MEN**

Help Mary and Joseph find the way to Bethlehem.

Section 3 | **21**

PAGES 22 AND 23: A BIRTHDAY

MATERIALS NEEDED

- crayons
- writing tablet
- Bible

Concept:

Jesus was born in Bethlehem.

Objective:

I can tell about Jesus.

Teacher Goal:

To teach the children about Jesus's birth.

Bible Reference:

Luke 2:6–20

Reading Integration:

Listening, main idea, picture interpretation, recalling details

Vocabulary:

stable, shepherds

GOD'S PROMISE TO MEN | Unit 6

A Birthday
(Luke 2:6–20)

When Mary and Joseph came to Bethlehem, they could not find a place to stay. Finally, they found a stable and stayed there.

While they were there, Jesus was born.

22 | Section 3

Teaching Pages 22 and 23:

Ask the children questions about the illustration.

"Who do they see in the picture?"

"Where is this picture?"

"Why is an animal in the picture?"

Read the title. Ask the children whose birthday they will read about.

Read the text and let the children expand the story from their knowledge of the Christmas story.

Read the Bible account and discuss more details of the story.

Read the direction. After the children complete their pictures, allow time for each child to discuss his picture.

Activities:

1. Have the children write two paragraphs about the Christmas story in their writing tablets. Allow time for each child to read his story.

2. Continue scrapbook.

3. Make a three-dimensional Christmas scene. Use the three-dimensional map of Bethlehem made in section one. Add a stable and figures made from tongue depressors or one-piece clothespins. Use scraps of material to clothe the figures. Use straw in the stable. Make shepherds and hills just outside of Bethlehem. Crushed green paper makes good hills.

   Add other details as the children wish. Provide ample space on a counter or table top.

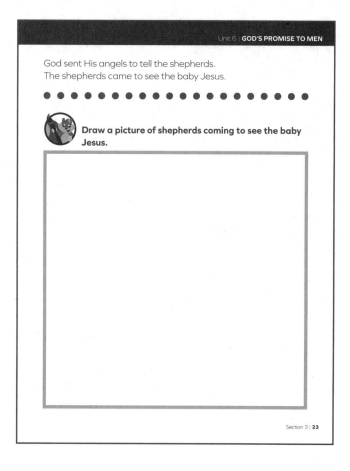

Unit 6 | **GOD'S PROMISE TO MEN**

God sent His angels to tell the shepherds.
The shepherds came to see the baby Jesus.

Draw a picture of shepherds coming to see the baby Jesus.

Section 3 | **23**

PAGE 24: THE TEMPLE

MATERIALS NEEDED

- Bible
- Worksheet 5

Concept:

Jesus is the Christ.

Objective:

I can tell about Jesus.

Teacher Goal:

To teach the children that some people knew who Jesus was even though He was a baby.

Bible Reference:

Luke 2:25–38

Reading Integration:

Main idea, listening, retelling story

Vocabulary:

Anna, Simeon, Temple

Teaching Page 24:

Explain to the children what the Temple was and the importance of the Temple to God's people.

Read the first paragraph. Explain why Jesus was taken to the Temple as a baby (Luke 1:21–24).

Read the second paragraph and discuss it with the children. Read the Bible account and discuss the illustration.

Activities:

1. Continue scrapbook.

2. Write a prayer thanking God for Jesus.

3. Do Worksheet 5.

   Follow the same directions and procedures as on Worksheet 4.

GOD'S PROMISE TO MEN | Unit 6

The Temple
(Luke 2:25-38)

When Jesus was still a baby,
Mary and Joseph took Him to the Temple.

An old man named Simeon saw Jesus.
He knew that Jesus was the Promised One.
An old widow named Anna saw Jesus, too.

They both thanked God for keeping His promise.

24 | Section 3

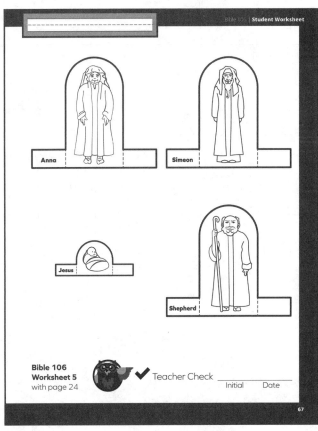

Bible 106 | **Student Worksheet**

Anna

Simeon

Jesus

Shepherd

**Bible 106
Worksheet 5**
with page 24

Teacher Check _____
Initial   Date

67

PAGE 25: ACTIVITY PAGE

MATERIALS NEEDED

- pencils
- Worksheet 6

Teaching Page 25:

Read the directions. Let the children do the page independently. Give help with vocabulary as needed.

Check together and discuss each answer in relation to the story.

Activity:

Do Worksheet 6.

Instruct the children to study the pictures carefully and to draw what happened next in the empty space.

Check by having the children tell the story for each picture. Accept any reasonable picture for the final box.

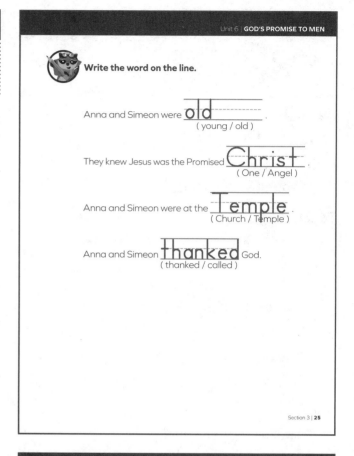

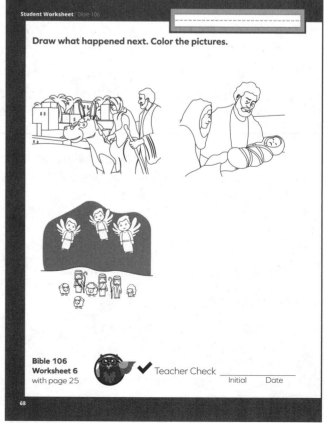

PAGE 26: WISE MEN AND A WICKED KING

MATERIALS NEEDED

- Bible
- Worksheet 7

Concept:

God protected Jesus.

Objective:

I can tell about Jesus.

Teacher Goal:

To teach the children how God watched over Jesus, Mary, and Joseph.

Bible Reference:

Matthew 2:1–23

Reading Integration:

Main idea, recalling details, retelling story

Vocabulary:

Herod, (Egypt)
Note: Vocabulary words in parentheses were previously introduced and are being reviewed.

Teaching Page 26:

Read the title. Ask the children what the title might mean.

Read the first paragraph. Read the corresponding Bible account and explain what the Wise Men's gifts were.

Read the second paragraph and the Bible account to the children.

GOD'S PROMISE TO MEN | Unit 6

Wise Men and a Wicked King
(Matthew 2:1–23)

God sent His star
to lead wise men to the baby Jesus.
They saw Him
and brought Him gifts.

A wicked king named Herod
tried to kill the baby Jesus.
An angel told Joseph
to take Jesus and Mary to Egypt.
Jesus was safe in Egypt.

26 | Section 3

Bible 106 | **Student Worksheet**

Wise Man

Wise Man

Wise Man

King Herod

**Bible 106
Worksheet 7**
with page 26

Teacher Check

_____ _____
Initial   Date

69

Ask questions such as these:

      "Where did the Wise Men come from?"

      "How did they know where to go?"

      "Why did they see King Herod?"

      "How did King Herod know about Jesus?"

      "Who told the Wise Men to go home a different way?"

      "Who wanted to hurt Jesus?"

      "How did God help Mary, Joseph, and Jesus?"

Activities:

1. Continue scrapbook.

2. Divide the children into three groups. Have one group act out the story of the Wise Men and King Herod (Matthew 2:1–10). Have the second group act out Matthew 2:11–15. Have the third group act out Matthew 2:19–23.

3. Do Worksheet 7.

Follow the same directions and procedures as on Worksheet 4.

PAGE 27: ACTIVITY PAGE

MATERIALS NEEDED

- crayons
- writing tablet

Teaching Page 27:

Read the direction.

Discuss the picture.

Let the children color the picture.

When they have finished, review the details of the story once again. Use the figures from Worksheets 4, 5, and 7 to help recall details.

Unit 6 | **GOD'S PROMISE TO MEN**

Color the picture.

Section 3 | **27**

PAGE 28: THE TEMPLE TEACHERS

MATERIALS NEEDED

- Bible
- paper
- crayons

Concept:

Jesus as a child.

Objective:

I can tell about Jesus.

Teacher Goal:

To teach the children what the Gospel says about the childhood of Jesus.

Bible Reference:

Luke 2:39–52

Reading Integration:

Main idea, listening, recalling details

Vocabulary:

Jerusalem

GOD'S PROMISE TO MEN | Unit 6

The Temple Teachers
(Luke 2:39–52)

When the wicked king died, Joseph, Mary, and Jesus went back to Nazareth.

When Jesus was twelve years old, He went to the Temple in Jerusalem with Mary and Joseph.

He surprised the teachers of the Temple because He knew so many things.

28 | Section 3

Teaching Page 28:

Read the title and the text to the children.

Read it again and discuss each paragraph.

Ask questions such as these:

"Where did Jesus, Mary, and Joseph go to live after King Herod died?"
"How old was Jesus when He went to the Temple with Mary and Joseph?"
"Where was the Temple?"
"What did Jesus do in the Temple?"
"Why?"

Read the Bible account and discuss the details of the story more fully.

Activities:

1. Continue scrapbook.
2. Have the children act out the story. If the children do well at dramatizing the stories, you may want to combine several from the LIFEPAC and have the children put on the story of Jesus, Mary, and Joseph for the parents. Parents could help children with lines and costumes.

3. Tape a long roll of shelf or butcher paper to the wall just high enough for the children to reach. Divide the paper into sections for each aspect of the LIFEPAC. Let the children plan a mural including all the events. Assign areas for each child to work when he has finished his other work.

PAGE 29: ACTIVITY PAGE

MATERIALS NEEDED

- pencils
- crayons
- map of the Land of Israel and Egypt during the time of the birth of Jesus

Teaching Page 29:

Read the direction.

Tell the children that you will read each direction only once. They may read them slightly later. Review the place names before you begin.

Read the first direction. Wait until the children have completed the item.

Read the second direction. Wait. Follow the same procedure for the last two directions.

You may want to have a map available so that the children can see how much to color for the last direction.

Activities:

1. If children have difficulty, make up simple map worksheets and give similar directions.

2. Finish pages of scrapbook.

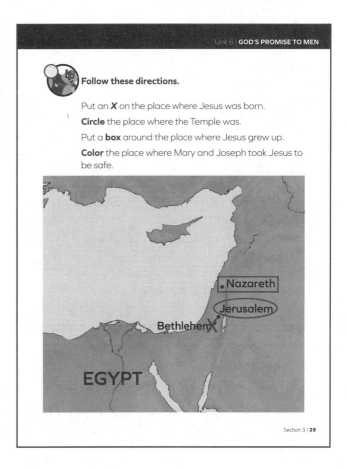

Unit 6 | **GOD'S PROMISE TO MEN**

Follow these directions.

Put an **X** on the place where Jesus was born.

Circle the place where the Temple was.

Put a **box** around the place where Jesus grew up.

Color the place where Mary and Joseph took Jesus to be safe.

Nazareth

Jerusalem

Bethlehem

EGYPT

Section 3 | **29**

PAGE 30: JESUS AS A BOY

Concept:

Jesus grows up.

Objective:

I can tell about Jesus.

Teacher Goal:

To teach the children what the Bible says about the childhood of Jesus.

Reading Integration:

Main idea, picture interpretation

Teaching Page 30:

Read the page and discuss the picture.

Ask the children what other things they know about Jesus's life. Tell them that they will learn many more things in Bible 107.

Activities:

1. Assemble scrapbook. Allow a short time each day for the children to talk about their books. Put the scrapbooks on display for parents, teachers, and children to see. When this display is finished, let the children take the scrapbooks home.

GOD'S PROMISE TO MEN | Unit 6

Jesus grew up in Nazareth.
He became a carpenter like Joseph.
He obeyed His parents in all things.

The Bible does not tell much about what Jesus did as a boy.
The Bible does say that Jesus grew in wisdom and stature, and in favour with God and man.

30 | Section 3

2. Review vocabulary names from the LIFEPAC. Put all the names in a box. Have each child pick a name and think of clues so that the class can guess what person, country, or town he is.

Example:

I helped Jesus, Mary, and Joseph.
They lived here when King Herod was trying to find Jesus.
What am I? (Egypt)

PAGE 31: ACTIVITY PAGE

MATERIALS NEEDED

• pencils
• Bible
• writing tablet

Teaching Page 31:

Read the memory verse. *Remember:* A cumulative list of Memory Verses is included. Explain words like *wisdom, stature, favor,* and *increased.* Have the children repeat the memory verse, find it in the Bible, and say it again.

Have the children complete both activities. You may want to duplicate the memory verse and send it home. Put room on the paper for the parents' signatures.

Discuss the memory verse. Ask the children how they have grown (increased) since they were very small. Ask them how they can grow in wisdom and in favor with God. Give each child an opportunity to speak.

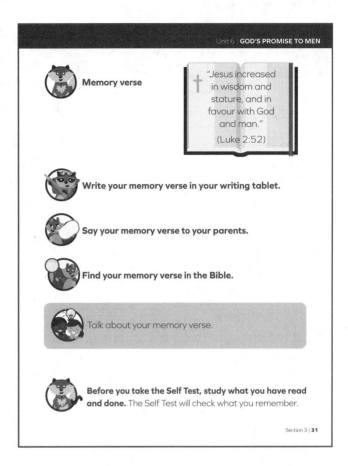

Activity:

Send all the memory verses home so that the parents will be able to help the children learn the verses.

The students should prepare for the Self Test. Ask the students to look over and read the Self Test but they should not write the answers to any questions. After looking over the Self Test the students should go to the beginning of the unit and reread the text and review the answers to the activities up to the Self Test.

The students are to complete the Self Test the next school day. This should be done under regular test conditions without allowing the students to look back. A good idea is to clip the pages together before the test.

PAGE 32: SELF TEST 3

MATERIALS NEEDED

• pencils

Concept:

Evaluation.

Objectives:

I can tell about God's promise.

I can tell how God kept His promise.

I can tell about Jesus.

Teacher Goal:

To check each child's progress.

Bible References:

All three memory verses and all other references.

Reading Integration:

Following written directions, recalling details

Vocabulary:

Review all vocabulary words.

Teaching Page 32:

Review all words and verses before beginning.

Read the directions and sentences if necessary.

Let the children complete the page independently.

Check immediately. Show each child where he has done well and where he must improve.

Review all concepts missed before going to the LIFEPAC Test.

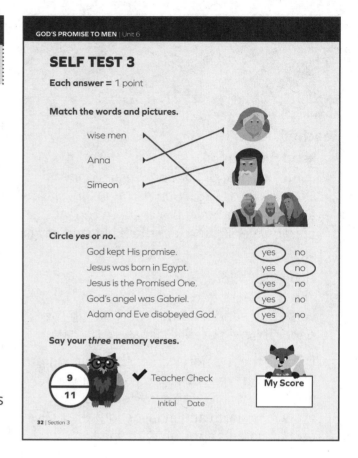

PAGE 33: TAKE HOME ACTIVITY PAGE

MATERIALS NEEDED

• crayons

Teaching Page 33:

Read the directions. Have the children find and circle the hidden pictures. Have them color the picture.

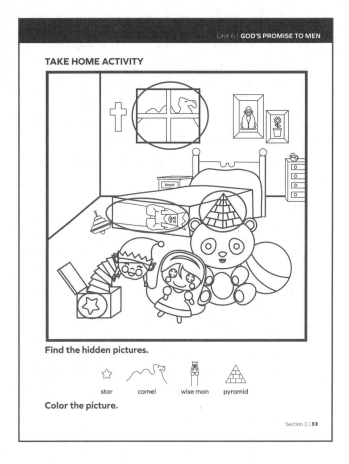

57

LIFEPAC TEST 106

Administer the test to the class as a group. Ask to have directions read or read them to the class. In either case, be sure that the children clearly understand. Put examples on the board if it seems necessary. Give ample time for each activity to be completed before going to the next.

Correct immediately and discuss with the child.

Review any concepts that have been missed.

Give those children who do not achieve the 80% score additional copies of the worksheets and a list of vocabulary words to study. A parent or a classroom helper should help in the review.

When the child is ready, give the Alternate LIFEPAC Test. Use the same procedure as for the LIFEPAC Test.

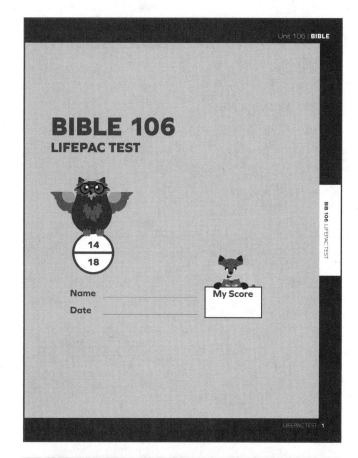

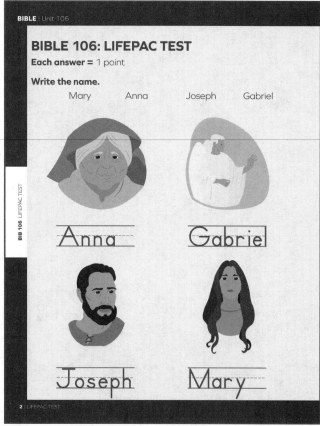

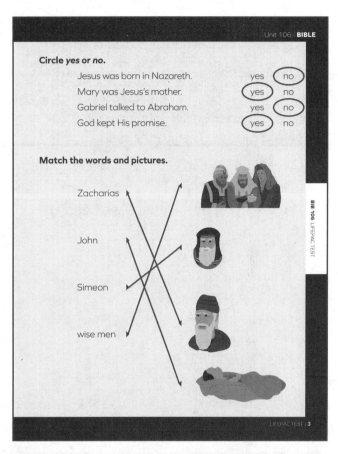

Circle *yes* or *no*.

Jesus was born in Nazareth.　　　　yes　(no)

Mary was Jesus's mother.　　　　(yes)　no

Gabriel talked to Abraham.　　　　yes　(no)

God kept His promise.　　　　(yes)　no

Match the words and pictures.

Zacharias

John

Simeon

wise men

LIFEPAC TEST | 3

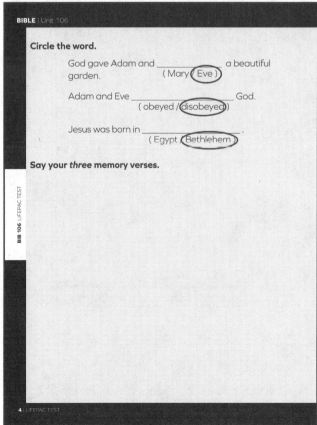

Circle the word.

God gave Adam and _____ a beautiful garden.
(Mary / (Eve))

Adam and Eve _____ God.
(obeyed / (disobeyed))

Jesus was born in _____ .
(Egypt / (Bethlehem))

Say your *three* memory verses.

4 | LIFEPAC TEST

ALTERNATE LIFEPAC TEST 106

Administer the test to the class as a group. Ask to have directions read or read them to the class. In either case, be sure that the children clearly understand. Put examples on the board if it seems necessary. Give ample time for each activity to be completed before going to the next.

Correct immediately and discuss with the child.

Review any concepts that have been missed.

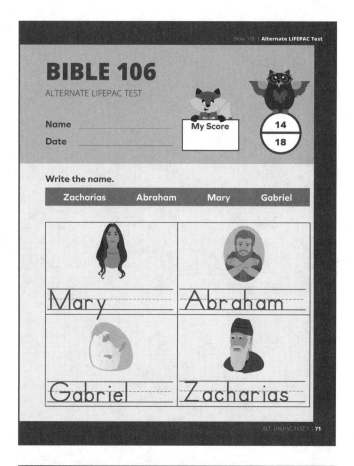

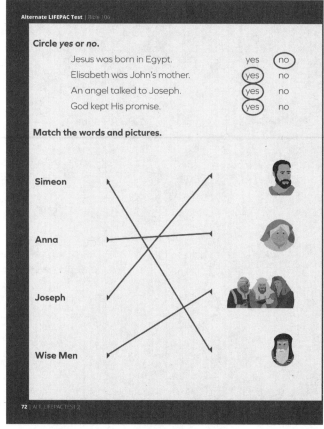

_____

Guess who I am.

I have a son named Isaac.

I am an old man.

God promised me something special.

My name begins with long /a/.

Who am I?

_____

- -

_____

Draw my picture.

**Bible 106
Worksheet 1**
with page 4

 ✔ Teacher Check _____
Initial   Date

Read the clues.
Write the words in the puzzle.

| made | nations | Abraham | save |

1. I have a son named Isaac.
2. All the _____ of the earth would be blessed.
3. Jesus came to _____ us from sin.
4. God _____ Adam and Eve.

Teacher Check _____
                    Initial   Date

Write *1*, *2*, *3*, and *4* to show what happened *first*, *second*, *third*, and *fourth*. Color the pictures.

Bible 106
Worksheet 3
with page 13

Teacher Check _____

Initial   Date

Gabriel

Joseph

Zacharias

Mary

Bible 106
Worksheet 4
with page 16

✔ Teacher Check _____

Initial   Date

Anna

Simeon

Jesus

Shepherd

✔ Teacher Check _____

Initial   Date

Draw what happened next. Color the pictures.

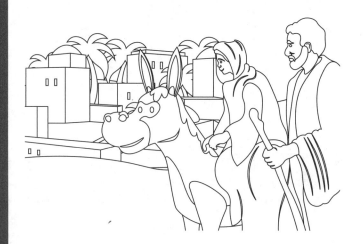

**Bible 106
Worksheet 6**
with page 25

✔ Teacher Check _____
                    Initial   Date

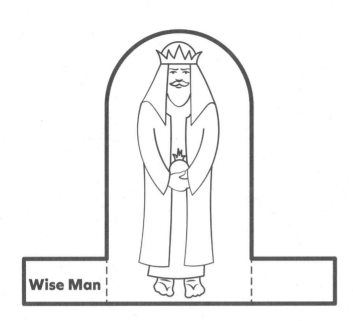

Wise Man

Wise Man

Wise Man

King Herod

Bible 106
Worksheet 7
with page 26

✔ Teacher Check _____

Initial   Date

BIBLE 106

ALTERNATE LIFEPAC TEST

Name _____

Date _____

My Score

14
—
18

Write the name.

Zacharias	Abraham	Mary	Gabriel

_____

_____

_____

_____

Circle *yes* or *no*.

Jesus was born in Egypt.	yes	no
Elisabeth was John's mother.	yes	no
An angel talked to Joseph.	yes	no
God kept His promise.	yes	no

Match the words and pictures.

Simeon ▶ ◀

Anna ▶ ◀

Joseph ▶ ◀

Wise Men ▶ ◀

Circle the word.

God asked _____ to be Jesus's mother.
Eve / Mary

Jesus grew up in _____ .
Bethlehem / Nazareth

The Promised One was _____ .
Jesus / John

Say your *three* memory verses.

BIBLE 107

Unit 7: Jesus, Our Savior

JESUS, OUR SAVIOR
BIBLE 107

Alpha Omega
PUBLICATIONS

804 N. 2nd Ave. E.
Rock Rapids, IA 51246-1759

Author:
Mary Ellen Quint, Ph.D.

Editor:
Rudolph Moore, Ph.D.

Consulting Editor:
John L. Booth, Th.D.

Revision Editor:
Alan Christopherson, M.S.

Media Credits:
Page 1: © Norberthos, iStock, Thinkstock;
25: © stockakia, iStock, Thinkstock.

| i

PAGE 1: JESUS, OUR SAVIOR

MATERIALS NEEDED

- pencils
- writing tablet

Concept:

God sent Jesus to save us.

Objective:

To introduce all the objectives.

Teacher Goal:

To teach the children what they will learn in this LIFEPAC.

Reading Integration:

Main idea

Vocabulary:

taught, died, rose, (Savior)
Note: Vocabulary words in parentheses were previously introduced and are being reviewed.

Unit 7 | JESUS, OUR SAVIOR

JESUS, OUR SAVIOR

In this LIFEPAC®,
you will learn more
about Jesus.
God sent His Son, Jesus,
to save us from sin.

Jesus taught people.
Jesus healed sick people.
Jesus died to save us.
Jesus rose from the dead.

Objectives

Read these objectives. They will tell what you will be able to do when you have finished this LIFEPAC®.

1. I can tell what Jesus taught.
2. I can tell about some people Jesus healed.
3. I can tell what Jesus did to save me from sin.

Introduction | **1**

Teaching Page 1:

Read the title or have a child read it.

Ask the children how many remember what the word Savior means.

Read the paragraph. Review the promise of God from Bible 106.

Read the second paragraph to the children. Tell them that in this LIFEPAC they will learn some of the things the Bible tells about Jesus's life.

Read the objectives. Have the children repeat them and copy them into their writing tablets.

1. JESUS TAUGHT

PAGES 2 AND 3

MATERIALS NEEDED

- pencils
- writing tablet
- Bible

Concept:

Jesus taught in many ways.

Objective:

I can tell what Jesus taught.

Teacher Goals:

To teach the children that we can learn many things and that the Gospels are the record of Christ's birth, ministry, death, and resurrection.

Reading Integration:

Main idea, interpreting pictures, recalling details

Vocabulary:

Gospel, Matthew, Mark, Luke, John, stories

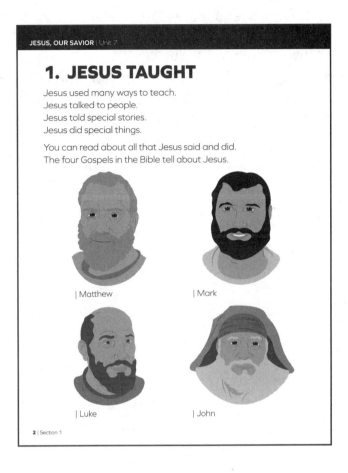

JESUS, OUR SAVIOR | Unit 7

1. JESUS TAUGHT

Jesus used many ways to teach.
Jesus talked to people.
Jesus told special stories.
Jesus did special things.

You can read about all that Jesus said and did.
The four Gospels in the Bible tell about Jesus.

| Matthew

| Mark

| Luke

| John

2 | Section 1

Teaching Pages 2 and 3:

Read the names under each picture. Ask the children if they know who these four men were. Tell them that these four men wrote the Gospels. Have them find the names and the four Gospels in the Bible.

Read the title. Tell the children that they will learn about different ways Jesus used to teach people about Himself and about His Father in Heaven.

Read the first paragraph and ask the children if they remember anything Jesus has said, any special stories He told, or any special things He did.

Read the second paragraph on page 2 and the two paragraphs on page 3 and discuss.

Read the directions on page 3. Urge the children to look back to page 2 if they cannot remember the picture for each name.

Check the writing tablet exercise by having the children read their answers.

Activities:

1. Read stories about Matthew, Mark, Luke, and John so that the children place them in perspective to the life of Jesus.

2. Have the children find the Gospel stories used in the LIFEPAC in their Bibles before each lesson.

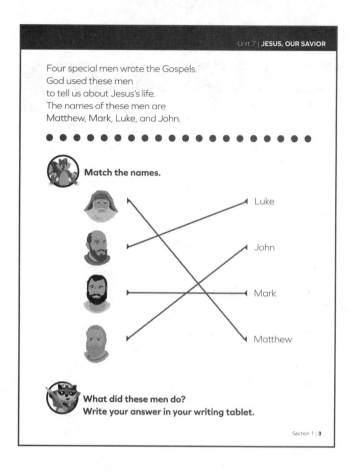

PAGES 4 AND 5: JESUS TALKED TO PEOPLE

MATERIALS NEEDED

- pencils
- writing tablet
- Worksheet 1

Concept:

Jesus taught by talking to people.

Objective:

I can tell what Jesus taught.

Teacher Goals:

To teach the children to recall some of the teachings they have learned and to learn a new verse from the Sermon on the Mount.

Bible Reference:

Matthew chapters 5–7

Reading Integration:

Main idea, listening, recalling details, speaking in a group

Vocabulary:

mountain, glorify, shine, (taught, enemies, father)
Note: Vocabulary words in parentheses were previously introduced and are being reviewed.

Teaching Pages 4 and 5:

Read the title. Have the children find Matthew chapters 5–7 in their Bibles.

Read the first paragraph. Ask the children if they remember what they learned in Bible 103 and 104 about things Jesus said.

Read the second paragraph and the paragraph at the top of page 5. Review the Lord's Prayer with the children and Jesus's command to love our enemies.

Read the first direction. Read Matthew 5:1–16 to the children and discuss the meaning of Jesus's message in terms the children can understand. Throughout the LIFEPAC continue to read and reread portions of the Sermon on the Mount to the children.

JESUS, OUR SAVIOR | Unit 7

Jesus Talked to People

(Matthew chapters 5–7)

Jesus taught people by talking to them.
He told them how they should live.
He told them how to pray.
He told them how to show love for God.

One day, Jesus talked from a mountain to many people.
He taught them many things.

4 | Section 1

Unit 7 | JESUS, OUR SAVIOR

You have learned parts of what He said that day.
You have learned the Lord's Prayer (Matthew 6:9–13).
You have learned that Jesus told you to love your enemies (Matthew 5:44).

● ●

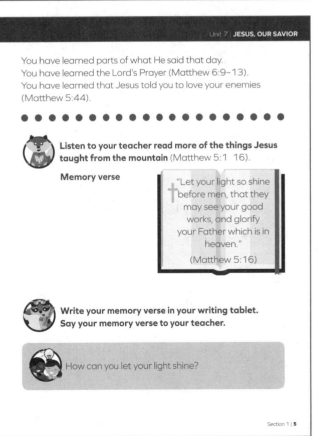

Listen to your teacher read more of the things Jesus taught from the mountain (Matthew 5:1–16).

Memory verse

"Let your light so shine before men, that they may see your good works, and glorify your Father which is in heaven."
(Matthew 5:16)

Write your memory verse in your writing tablet. Say your memory verse to your teacher.

How can you let your light shine?

Section 1 | **5**

Read the memory verse to the children. Answer any questions and explain any words they do not understand. The length of this verse makes it difficult to learn all at once. Work on it with the children through-out Section 1 so that they can say it from memory by the first self test.

Sending a copy of the verse home to the parents will allow the children to work on the memory verse at home.

Have the children write their verse in their writing tablets. Check for accuracy, penmanship, and neatness. Have them rewrite it if necessary.

Discuss the question in small groups or as a class. Ask the children what good works they can do to let their light shine and to glorify their heavenly Father.

Activities:

1. Have the children use the good works in the "Show your love" box (Bible 104) as a beginning for ideas on letting their light shine. Add new ideas to the box. Review the reasons for the box and for doing good to others.

2. Do Worksheet 1.

    Read the directions. Go over the words in the box with the children.

    Let the children complete the page independently.

    Check together and read two or three times to help the children learn and understand the verse.

3. Have the children draw pictures of ways they can let their lights shine. Make a bulletin board display for the pictures.

PAGE 6: JESUS TOLD SPECIAL STORIES

MATERIALS NEEDED

- pencils
- crayons
- Bible
- drawing paper
- writing tablet

Concept:

Parables are special stories that teach a lesson.

Objective:

I can tell what Jesus taught.

Teacher Goal:

To teach the children what a parable is and how Jesus used parables to teach.

Bible Reference:

Matthew 13:3–23

Reading Integration:

Main idea, vocabulary development

Vocabulary:

parable, lesson, (taught, stories)
Note: Vocabulary words in parentheses were previously introduced and are being reviewed.

JESUS, OUR SAVIOR | Unit 7

Jesus Told Special Stories
(Matthew 13:3–23)

Sometimes Jesus taught by telling special stories. These special stories are called parables. Parables teach a lesson.

You will learn one parable. Your teacher will read more parables to you.

6 | Section 1

Teaching Page 6:

Read the title to the children. Ask how many know some of the special stories Jesus told. Some may be familiar with the Good Shepherd, the prodigal son, the good Samaritan (Bible 104), and so on. Let the children discuss and share the stories they know.

Read page 6. Emphasize that these special stories that Jesus used to teach people are called parables.

Discuss the illustration. Tell the children that they will learn a story that Jesus told about a man who planted some seeds.

Activities:

1. Take time to read some of the parables discussed by the children.

2. Begin a parable book as a class project. Make one large class book or have the children work as a class on individual books to take home. The children can draw or cut out pictures to illustrate each parable. They can write a few sentences about each on writing tablet paper and paste this text under the pictures. Teach them to write the Bible reference for each parable.

3. Have small groups of children act out their favorite parables for the class. Have the class guess which parable has been chosen.

PAGE 7: ACTIVITY PAGE

MATERIALS NEEDED

- pencils
- writing tablet

Teaching Page 7:

Read the directions. Do the first activity together if the children need help. Urge them to look on page 6 for help. Read all the sentences together when the right word has been circled.

Read the second direction. Let the children complete the activity. Check for accuracy.

Do the third activity together.

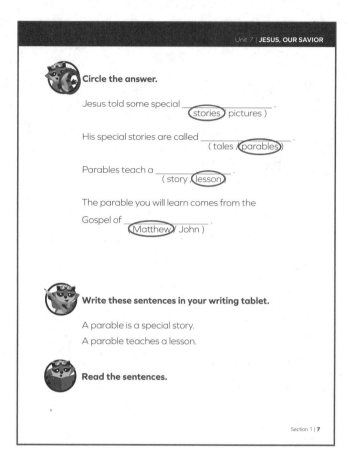

PAGES 8 AND 9: PARABLE OF THE SOWER

MATERIALS NEEDED

- pencils
- Bible
- writing table
- Worksheet 2

Concept:

The Word of God falls on many ears, but not all listen and grow.

Objective:

I can tell what Jesus taught.

Teacher Goal:

To teach the children about parables and the lessons they teach.

Bible References:

Matthew 13:3–8, 18–23

Reading Integration:

Listening, picture interpretation, drawing conclusions, speaking in a group

Vocabulary:

sower, (parable, seeds)
Note: Vocabulary words in parentheses were previously introduced and are being reviewed.

Teaching Pages 8 and 9:

Read the title. Explain what a sower is.

Discuss each picture as you read (or have a child read) the sentences that accompany it. Draw on the children's own experiences with gardening if possible.

Discuss the two questions. Let each child contribute some ideas on each question. Read Matthew 13:18–23 after the children have expressed their ideas. Discuss the interpretation of the parable given in Matthew in language the children will understand. Ask the children how they can grow to be good and strong in God's Word just as the seed that fell on good ground.

JESUS, OUR SAVIOR | Unit 7

The Parable of the Sower
(Matthew 13:3–8, 18–23)

A man went out to plant some seeds.

Some seeds fell by the wayside. The birds came and ate them.

Some seeds fell on stony ground. They grew fast, but the sun burned them.

Some seeds fell in the thorns. The thorns grew, but the seedlings had no room to grow.

8 | Section 1

Unit 7 | JESUS, OUR SAVIOR

Some seeds fell on good ground. They grew and grew. They brought forth fruit.

The story of the sower is a parable.

What lesson does this story teach?
What do all the different soils stand for?

Listen to your teacher read Matthew 13:18–23.

Section 1 | 9

Activities:

1. Add the parable of the sower to the parable book.

2. Have the children write one paragraph in their writing tablets to tell how they can grow strong in God's Word. Help with spelling. Allow time for the children to share their paragraphs.

3. Do Worksheet 2.

    This Worksheet may be used in school or used to send home for a parent-child review of the story.

    Have the children recall the story by following the pictures.

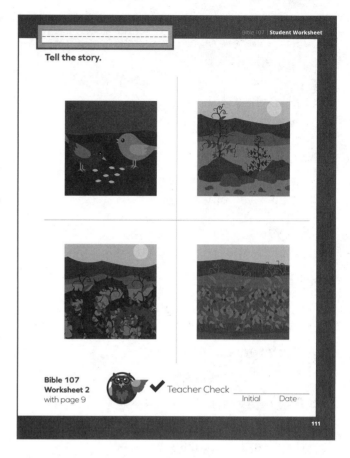

84

PAGES 10, 11, AND 12: JESUS DID SPECIAL THINGS

MATERIALS NEEDED

- Bible
- Worksheet 3

Concept:

Jesus did special things.

Objective:

I can tell what Jesus taught.

Teacher Goal:

To teach the children what a miracle is.

Bible References:

Mark 4:36–41; Matthew 8:23–27

Reading Integration:

Main idea, recalling details, retelling story, sequence

Vocabulary:

miracle, storm, still

Teaching Pages 10, 11, and 12:

Read the title. Ask the children if they can remember some of the special things Jesus did. Let the children share the stories of any miracles they may remember.

Read the text. Tell the children that sometimes Jesus taught people by doing rather than by speaking. The very special things He did to show God's love and power are called miracles.

Discuss the illustration on page 10. Tell the children they will learn about something special that Jesus did one day at sea.

Read the story on pages 11 and 12 through once as the children listen. Read it again as the children follow along. Stop after each paragraph to discuss the content and the illustrations.

JESUS, OUR SAVIOR | Unit 7

Jesus Did Special Things
(Mark 4:36–41; Matthew 8:23–27)

Sometimes Jesus did special things.
He did them to teach others more about God.
These special things were called miracles.

10 | Section 1

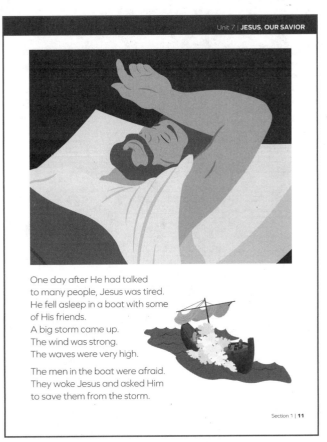

Unit 7 | **JESUS, OUR SAVIOR**

One day after He had talked
to many people, Jesus was tired.
He fell asleep in a boat with some
of His friends.
A big storm came up.
The wind was strong.
The waves were very high.

The men in the boat were afraid.
They woke Jesus and asked Him
to save them from the storm.

Section 1 | 11

Ask the children what they think Jesus had taught his friends by stopping the storm.

Help the children find either account of this miracle in their Bibles. Read the story to them from the Bible.

Activities:

1. Have the children act out this story.

2. Read Bible accounts of other miracles Jesus worked to the children.

3. Make a bulletin board of SPECIAL THINGS JESUS DID. Have the children draw pictures or write paragraphs about other miracles of Jesus.

4. Do Worksheet 3.

   Read the directions. Let the children complete the picture independently. Have the children take turns retelling the story.

JESUS, OUR SAVIOR | Unit 7

Jesus asked them
why they were afraid,
why they had so little faith.

Jesus stood up.
He told the sea and the winds
to be still. The storm stopped.
The sea grew still.

The men were surprised.
Jesus had taught them more
about God and Himself.

12 | Section 1

Student Worksheet | Bible 107

Follow the dots. Color the pictures. Tell the story.

Bible 107
Worksheet 3
with page 12

Teacher Check _____
Initial   Date

112

PAGE 13: ACTIVITY PAGE

MATERIALS NEEDED

• pencils

Teaching Page 13:

Read the first direction. Do the activity together if necessary.

Read the second direction. Let the children do this activity independently. Check together by having the children retell the story as they give their answers.

Review the story and the lesson that Jesus taught His friends. Give each child an opportunity to contribute to the discussion.

The students should prepare for the Self Test. Ask the students to look over and read the Self Test but they should not write the answers to any questions. After looking over the Self Test the students should go to the beginning of the unit and reread the text and review the answers to the activities up to the Self Test.

The students are to complete the Self Test the next school day. This should be done under regular test conditions without allowing the students to look back. A good idea is to clip the pages together before the test.

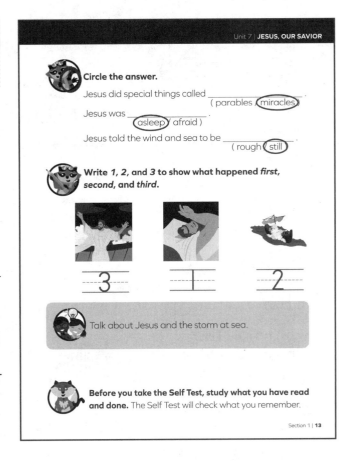

Unit 7 | **JESUS, OUR SAVIOR**

Circle the answer.

Jesus did special things called _____ .
(parables ⟨miracles⟩)

Jesus was _____ .
(⟨asleep⟩ afraid)

Jesus told the wind and sea to be _____ .
(rough ⟨still⟩)

Write 1, 2, and 3 to show what happened first, second, and third.

_3_   _1_   _2_

Talk about Jesus and the storm at sea.

Before you take the Self Test, study what you have read and done. The Self Test will check what you remember.

Section 1 | **13**

87

PAGE 14: SELF TEST 1

MATERIALS NEEDED

• pencils

Concept:

Evaluation.

Objective:

I can tell what Jesus taught.

Teacher Goal:

To check each child's progress.

Bible References:

Review memory verse and all other references.

Reading Integration:

Following written directions, recalling details, sequence

Vocabulary:

Review all vocabulary words.

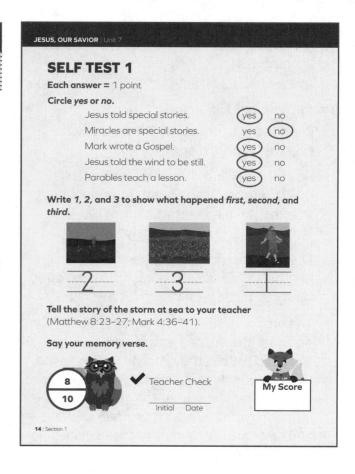

Teaching Page 14:

Read the directions and the sentences for those who need help. Let the children complete the page independently.

Check immediately and show each child where he has done well and where he needs to work harder.

Review any concepts missed individually or in small groups.

2.   JESUS HEALED

PAGE 15

Concept:

Jesus helped many people by healing.

Objective:

I can tell about some people Jesus healed.

Teacher Goals:

To teach the children that God can work through people's sickness and that Jesus could teach by healing.

Reading Integration:

Main idea

Vocabulary:

healed, (sick, miracles)
Note: Vocabulary words in parentheses were previously introduced and are being reviewed.

Teaching Page 15:

Read the title. Ask the children what it means to *heal* someone.

Read the page. Ask the children if they remember any stories from the Bible about sick people that Jesus healed.

Go immediately to page 16.

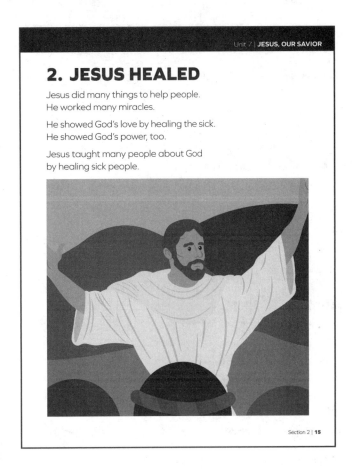

Unit 7 | **JESUS, OUR SAVIOR**

2. JESUS HEALED

Jesus did many things to help people. He worked many miracles.

He showed God's love by healing the sick. He showed God's power, too.

Jesus taught many people about God by healing sick people.

Section 2 | 15

PAGES 16 AND 17: THE CRIPPLED MAN

MATERIALS NEEDED

• Bible

Concept:

Jesus healed a crippled man.

Objective:

I can tell about some people Jesus healed.

Teacher Goal:

To teach the children that faith and confession of sins are important parts of being healed.

Bible Reference:

Mark 2:3–12

Reading Integration:

Main idea, listening, retelling story

Vocabulary:

crippled, roof

Teaching Pages 16 and 17:

Read the title. Ask the children what *crippled* means.

Discuss each picture and its text separately.

Ask the children why they think faith and confession of sins were important. Ask why Jesus was pleased with the faith of the man's friends.

Explain to the children the construction of houses at that time, why the roof had a hole, why the men could easily climb up on the roof, and so on.

Activities:

1. Have the children take turns acting out the story.

2. Have the children draw a picture of the crippled man after Jesus healed him.

Jesus Made the Crippled Man Walk
(Mark 2:3–12)

One day, four men brought a crippled man to see Jesus.

Many people were around Jesus. The men could not get to Jesus. The four men had to lower the crippled man down through the roof.

16 | Section 2

Unit 7 | **JESUS, OUR SAVIOR**

When Jesus saw the man, He was pleased with the faith of the man's friends. He forgave the man's sins.

Jesus told the man, "Arise, and take up your bed, and go to your house." The man got up, took up his bed, and walked home.

Section 2 | **17**

PAGE 18: ACTIVITY PAGE

MATERIALS NEEDED

• pencils

Teaching Page 18:

Read the directions. Help with the sentence vocabulary if necessary.

Give each child a chance to tell what happened next. Use aides or volunteers if possible so that each child has an opportunity to retell the story and not simply to repeat what another child has said.

Write the answer.

The crippled man could not **walk**
(sleep (walk)

Jesus forgave the man's **sins**
(sins) goods)

The man walked to his **home**
(home) bed)

Tell what happened next.

18 | Section 2

91

PAGE 19: ACTIVITY PAGE

MATERIALS NEEDED

| • pencils | • Worksheet 4 |
| • writing tablet | |

Vocabulary:

lame

Teaching Page 19:

The memory verse on this page is difficult for both its length and its vocabulary length and its vocabulary. This verse should be learned gradually through Section 2, *NOT* all at once. If some children cannot learn the entire verse, allow them to memorize only part of it.

Read the verse three times with the children. Explain any words they do not understand.

Have them write the verse at least once in their writing tablets. They may have to do this over a period of time after other work has been completed.

Do not expect them to say the verse from memory at this time.

Spend as much time as needed to discuss the verse.

Let each child ask questions or add comments. Ask the children to tell ways they can help the blind, the lame, the deaf, the sick, and the poor around them. Ask them what lesson they think Jesus taught the people when He healed the crippled man.

Activities:

1. Send a copy of the memory verse home for parent-child study.

2. Do Worksheet 4.

   Read the directions and all words and phrases.

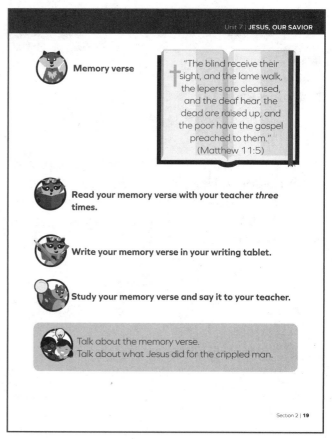

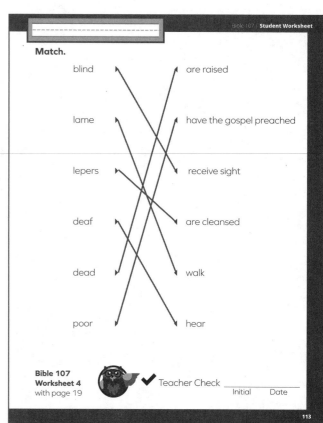

Let the children do the sheet independently. Tell them to refer to the memory verse on page 19 if they need help.

Check together by reading the memory verse and by matching each word as it occurs in the verse.

PAGES 20 AND 21: THE BLIND MAN

MATERIALS NEEDED

- crayons
- Bible

Concept:

Jesus healed a blind man.

Objective:

I can tell about some people Jesus healed.

Teacher Goal:

To teach the children that Jesus taught people of God's power by healing.

Bible Reference:

John chapter 9

Reading Integration:

Main idea, listening, recalling details, speaking in a group

Vocabulary:

blind, mud

JESUS, OUR SAVIOR | Unit 7

Jesus Made the Blind Man See
(John 9)

One day, Jesus met
a man who was blind.
The man had been blind
since he was born.

Jesus made mud and
put it on the man's eyes.
He told the man
to wash in a pool of water.

20 | Section 2

Teaching Pages 20 and 21:

Read the title.

Ask the children to read the story silently. Give help with vocabulary.

Ask these questions:

"Who did Jesus meet one day?" (a blind man)

"How long had the man been blind?" (since birth)

"What did Jesus do to the man's eyes?" (put mud on them)

"What did Jesus tell the man to do?" (wash in a pool of water)

"What happened when the man washed his eyes?" (he could see)

Read the story in John chapter 9 to the children from the Bible. Stress the importance of this miracle to show Jesus's power.

Read the direction on page 21. When the children have completed their pictures, allow time to discuss each picture and the discussion sentence.

Activities:

1. Read stories about blind people and talk about the gift of sight. Review concepts taught in History & Geography 102 about ways in which blind people communicate.

2. Let the children act out the story of the blind man.

3. Continue work on the memory verse.

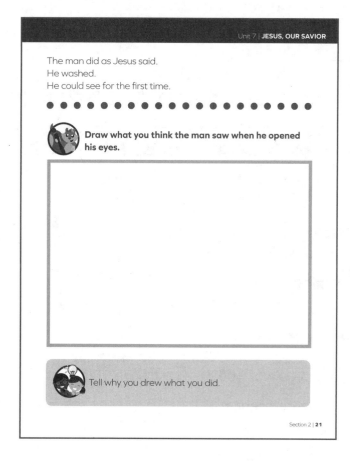

PAGE 22: THE DEAF MAN

MATERIALS NEEDED

• Bible

Concept:

Jesus healed a deaf man.

Objective:

I can tell about some people Jesus healed.

Teacher Goal:

To teach the children that Jesus's miracles showed His power.

Bible Reference:

Mark 7:32–37

Reading Integration:

Main idea

Vocabulary:

deaf

Teaching Page 22:

Read the title. Review what children have already learned about the deaf (History & Geography 102).

Read the first paragraph. Ask the children why a person who cannot hear may have trouble speaking. (cannot hear the speech sounds)

Read the second and third paragraphs. Ask the children why the people were amazed. Ask them what lesson Jesus taught with this miracle.

Activities:

1. Continue work on memory verse.

2. Read the Bible account of this story. Read it a second time and have the class act it out as you read.

JESUS, OUR SAVIOR | Unit 7

Jesus Made the Deaf Man Hear
(Mark 7:32–37)

Jesus healed a deaf man, too.
The man could not hear.
The man could not speak very well.

Jesus touched the man.
Jesus prayed.
The man could hear.
The man could speak plainly.

All the people who heard and saw what Jesus did were amazed.

22 | Section 2

PAGE 23: ACTIVITY PAGE

MATERIALS NEEDED

- pencils

Teaching Page 23:

Read the directions and the sentences for those who need help.

Check the first activity together reviewing the story as you do.

Have those children who are ready recite their memory verse. Children who have memorized the verse may work with those who have not yet learned the whole verse.

Spend some time on the discussion questions. Let each child contribute ideas. Ask the children how they can help someone who is deaf. Use the discussion to review concepts for the test.

The students should prepare for the Self Test. Ask the students to look over and read the Self Test but they should not write the answers to any questions. After looking over the Self Test the students should go to the beginning of the unit and reread the text and review the answers to the activities up to the Self Test.

The students are to complete the Self Test the next school day. This should be done under regular test conditions without allowing the students to look back. A good idea is to clip the pages together before the test.

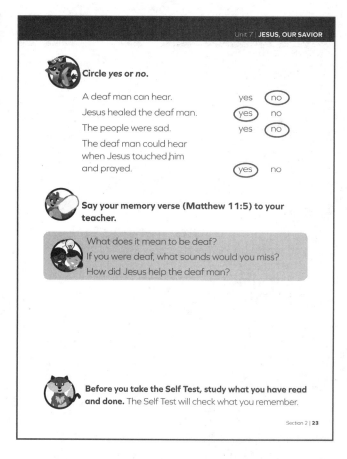

Unit 7 | **JESUS, OUR SAVIOR**

Circle *yes* or *no*.

A deaf man can hear.	yes	(no)
Jesus healed the deaf man.	(yes)	no
The people were sad.	yes	(no)
The deaf man could hear when Jesus touched him and prayed.	(yes)	no

Say your memory verse (Matthew 11:5) to your teacher.

What does it mean to be deaf?
If you were deaf, what sounds would you miss?
How did Jesus help the deaf man?

Before you take the Self Test, study what you have read and done. The Self Test will check what you remember.

Section 2 | **23**

PAGE 24: SELF TEST 2

MATERIALS NEEDED

• pencils

Concept:

Evaluation.

Objectives:

I can tell what Jesus taught.

I can tell about some people Jesus healed.

Teacher Goal:

To check each child's progress.

Bible References:

Review both memory verses and all stories.

Reading Integration:

Following written directions, sequence, recalling details

Vocabulary:

Review all vocabulary words.

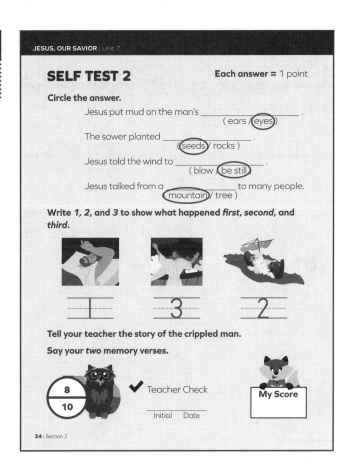

Teaching Page 24:

Read all directions and sentences for those who need help. Slower children should not be required to recite both memory verses. One will be sufficient.

Check immediately and go over the page individually.

Review any concept missed. If a child needs further help have an aide or parent review the LIFEPAC text and activities with him.

3. JESUS CAN SAVE US FROM SIN

PAGE 25

MATERIALS NEEDED

• Bible 106

Concept:

Jesus can save us from sin.

Objective:

I can tell what Jesus did to save me from sin.

Teacher Goal:

To teach the children that Jesus is the Savior, the Promised One.

Reading Integration:

Main idea, picture interpretation, recalling details

Vocabulary:

(Adam, Eve)
Note: Vocabulary words in parentheses were previously introduced and are being reviewed.

Unit 7 | **JESUS, OUR SAVIOR**

3. JESUS CAN SAVE US FROM SIN

God promised Adam and Eve He would send someone to save people from sin.

God sent His Son. God sent Jesus. Jesus came to save people from sin.

Section 3 | **25**

Teaching Page 25:

Discuss the illustrations. Review God's promise and the birth of Jesus (Bible 106).

Read the text or have a child read it.

Tell the children that in this part they will learn what Jesus did to save all people from sin.

PAGES 26 AND 27: JESUS DIED

MATERIALS NEEDED

- pencils
- Bibles
- writing tablet

Concept:

Jesus died to save us.

Objective:

I can tell what Jesus did to save me from sin.

Bible References:

Matthew 27; Mark 15; Luke 23; John 19

Reading Integration:

Main idea, recalling details, speaking in a group

Vocabulary:

cross, (Jerusalem, died)
Note: Vocabulary words in parentheses were previously introduced and are being reviewed.

Teaching Pages 26 and 27:

Ask the children what they see in the illustration. Ask them if they know what the illustration shows.

Read the title and text as the children listen. Reread the text and pause for discussion after each paragraph. If you wish, read from one of the Gospel accounts to fill out the details of the Last Supper, the garden, the arrest, trial, and crucifixion of Jesus.

Do not dwell too long on the exact nature of the suffering of Christ (some children can become very frightened by this).

Emphasize that Jesus had to die to save us.

Emphasize also the importance of asking Jesus into their lives.

Read the direction. Let the children do the activity. Check together.

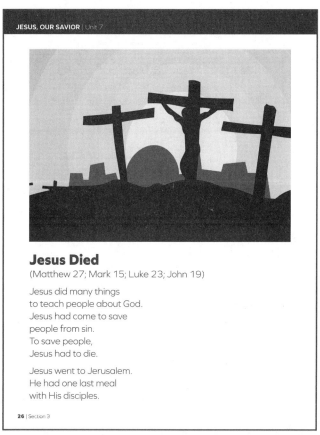

JESUS, OUR SAVIOR | Unit 7

Jesus Died
(Matthew 27; Mark 15; Luke 23; John 19)

Jesus did many things
to teach people about God.
Jesus had come to save
people from sin.
To save people,
Jesus had to die.

Jesus went to Jerusalem.
He had one last meal
with His disciples.

26 | Section 3

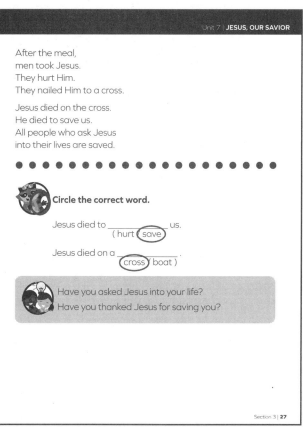

Unit 7 | **JESUS, OUR SAVIOR**

After the meal,
men took Jesus.
They hurt Him.
They nailed Him to a cross.

Jesus died on the cross.
He died to save us.
All people who ask Jesus
into their lives are saved.

● ● ● ● ● ● ● ● ● ● ● ● ● ● ● ● ● ● ●

Circle the correct word.

Jesus died to _____ us.
(hurt save)

Jesus died on a _____ .
(cross boat)

Have you asked Jesus into your life?
Have you thanked Jesus for saving you?

Section 3 | **27**

Allow time for each child to reflect on the discussion questions. Do not press for answers, but let children volunteer to answer these questions.

Activity:

Have the children write a thank-you prayer in their writing tablets. They can thank God for sending Jesus to save them or thank Jesus for dying to save them.

PAGES 28 AND 29: JESUS ROSE

MATERIALS NEEDED

- pencils
- writing tablet
- Bible
- Worksheet 5

Concept:

Jesus rose from the dead.

Objective:

I can tell what Jesus did to save me from sin.

Teacher Goal:

To teach the children about the Resurrection.

Bible References:

Matthew 28:1–8; Mark 16:1–13; Luke 24:1–48; John chapters 20 & 21

Reading Integration:

Main idea, speaking in a group, recalling details

Vocabulary:

third, risen, (rose)
Note: Vocabulary words in parentheses were previously introduced and are being reviewed.

Teaching Pages 28 and 29:

Read the story of Mary's meeting with Jesus after the Resurrection (John 20:11–18) and discuss the story and the illustration on page 28.

Read the text on pages 28 and 29. Reread and discuss each paragraph. Use the Bible accounts to fill in details and specific stories.

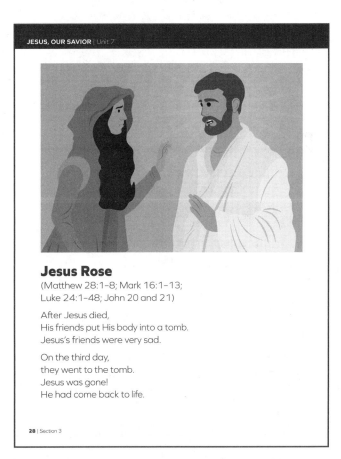

JESUS, OUR SAVIOR | Unit 7

Jesus Rose

(Matthew 28:1–8; Mark 16:1–13; Luke 24:1–48; John 20 and 21)

After Jesus died,
His friends put His body into a tomb.
Jesus's friends were very sad.

On the third day,
they went to the tomb.
Jesus was gone!
He had come back to life.

28 | Section 3

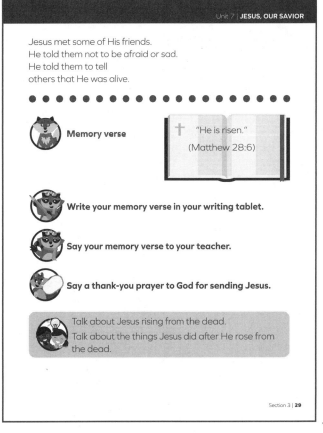

Unit 7 | JESUS, OUR SAVIOR

Jesus met some of His friends.
He told them not to be afraid or sad.
He told them to tell
others that He was alive.

Memory verse

✝ "He is risen."
(Matthew 28:6)

Write your memory verse in your writing tablet.

Say your memory verse to your teacher.

Say a thank-you prayer to God for sending Jesus.

Talk about Jesus rising from the dead.
Talk about the things Jesus did after He rose from the dead.

Section 3 | 29

Emphasize the importance of the Resurrection to all Christians and the joy all Christians should express. Help the children understand that Easter is the most important day of the entire year for a Christian (even more important than Christmas) because it is the day we all celebrate Christ's resurrection from the dead.

Read the memory verse. Have the children repeat it after you.

Read the directions and allow time for the children to complete the activities.

Read the discussion sentences. Ask the children what Jesus taught by rising from the dead. Read more Bible accounts of the things Jesus did and said between the Resurrection and His return to His Father. Emphasize that Jesus continued to teach by saying and doing special things just as He had done before His death. Ask the children what one special thing Jesus did often after His Resurrection (His ability to appear and disappear among His disciples).

Activity:

Do Worksheet 5.

Read the directions.

Discuss the illustration with the children.

Have them write their answer on the line. Check together and use as a review of the events leading up to and following the Resurrection.

Let the children color the picture when their other work is finished.

PAGES 30 AND 31: JESUS WILL COME AGAIN

MATERIALS NEEDED

• pencils

Concept:

Jesus will come again.

Objective:

I can tell what Jesus did to save me from sin.

Teacher Goal:

To teach the children of Jesus's promise to return someday.

Bible References:

Matthew 28:9–20; Mark 16:14–20;
Luke 24:49–53; John 21:23

Reading Integration:

Main idea, recalling details

Vocabulary:

return, (rose)
Note: Vocabulary words in parentheses were previously introduced and are being reviewed.

Teaching Pages 30 and 31:

Have a child read the title. Ask the children if they know what this title means.

Read the first paragraph or have a child read it.

Read the second paragraph. Ask the children how Jesus's friends must have felt when He told them He was leaving them. Ask how they must have felt when He told them He would come again someday.

Read the sentence at the top of page 31. Read the paragraph and explain any words in the quotation that the children do not understand.

Read the final sentence or have a child read it. Ask the children to tell ways that they can do what Jesus said.

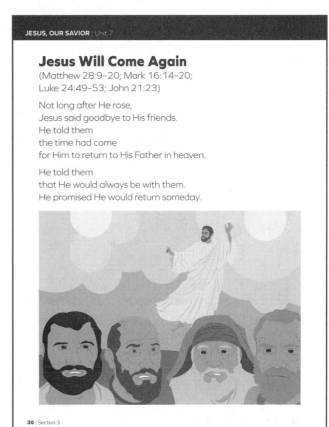

JESUS, OUR SAVIOR | Unit 7

Jesus Will Come Again

(Matthew 28:9–20; Mark 16:14–20;
Luke 24:49–53; John 21:23)

Not long after He rose,
Jesus said goodbye to His friends.
He told them
the time had come
for Him to return to His Father in heaven.

He told them
that He would always be with them.
He promised He would return someday.

30 | Section 3

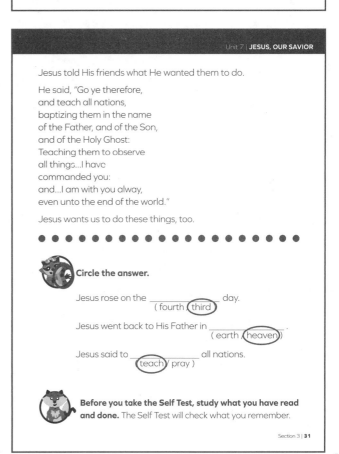

Unit 7 | JESUS, OUR SAVIOR

Jesus told His friends what He wanted them to do.

He said, "Go ye therefore,
and teach all nations,
baptizing them in the name
of the Father, and of the Son,
and of the Holy Ghost:
Teaching them to observe
all things...I have
commanded you:
and...I am with you alway,
even unto the end of the world."

Jesus wants us to do these things, too.

● ●

Circle the answer.

Jesus rose on the _____ day.
(fourth / third)

Jesus went back to His Father in _____ .
(earth / heaven)

Jesus said to _____ all nations.
(teach / pray)

Before you take the Self Test, study what you have read and done. The Self Test will check what you remember.

Section 3 | 31

Read the direction. Let the children do the activity independently. Help with vocabulary as needed.

Check together and discuss as a review of Section 3.

Activities:

1. As a review of the LIFEPAC, take a day or two of class to make a booklet on the LIFE OF JESUS. Have the children work in small groups to prepare sections of Jesus's life from Bible 106 and 107. The book could contain a section on Jesus as a child, a section on things Jesus said, a section on parables, a section on miracles, a section on His death and resurrection. Children can draw pictures and write story summaries for each section.

   The booklet can be used throughout the school year, but especially during the Easter season.

2. As a review of the LIFEPAC, have the children act out the LIFE OF JESUS selecting from the stories they have learned and discussed. This little play could be staged for another class or for the parents.

The students should prepare for the Self Test. Ask the students to look over and read the Self Test but they should not write the answers to any questions. After looking over the Self Test the students should go to the beginning of the unit and reread the text and review the answers to the activities up to the Self Test.

The students are to complete the Self Test the next school day. This should be done under regular test conditions without allowing the students to look back. A good idea is to clip the pages together before the test.

PAGES 32 AND 33: SELF TEST 3

MATERIALS NEEDED

• pencils

Concept:

Evaluation.

Objectives:

I can tell what Jesus taught.

I can tell about some people Jesus healed.

I can tell what Jesus did to save me from sin.

Teacher Goal:

To check each child's progress.

Bible References:

Bible memory verses and all stories.

Reading Integration:

Following written directions, recalling details, sequence

Vocabulary:

Review all vocabulary.

Teacher Pages 32 and 33:

Read the directions and sentences on page 32. When the children have finished page 32, read the directions and sentences on page 33. Slower children should only be required to recite two memory verses (one from Section 3 and one of the two long verses).

Check immediately and review the pages with each child.

Provide review and drill on concepts missed before giving the LIFEPAC Test.

Activity:

Complete all activities and books for the LIFEPAC as review for the LIFEPAC Test.

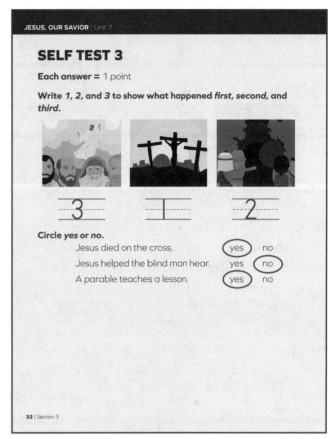

LIFEPAC TEST 107

Administer the test to the class as a group. Ask to have directions read or read them to the class. In either case, be sure that the children clearly understand. Put examples on the board if it seems necessary. Give ample time for each activity to be completed before going to the next.

Correct immediately and discuss with the child.

Review any concepts that have been missed.

Give those children who do not achieve the 80% score additional copies of the worksheets and a list of vocabulary words to study. A parent or a classroom helper should help in the review.

When the child is ready, give the Alternate LIFEPAC Test. Use the same procedure as for the LIFEPAC Test.

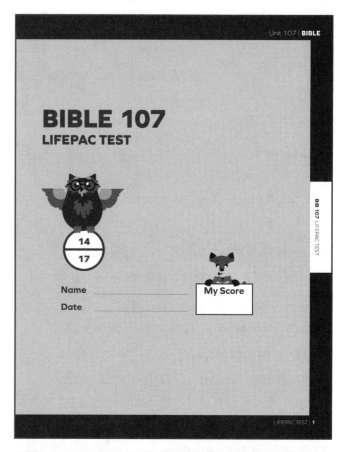

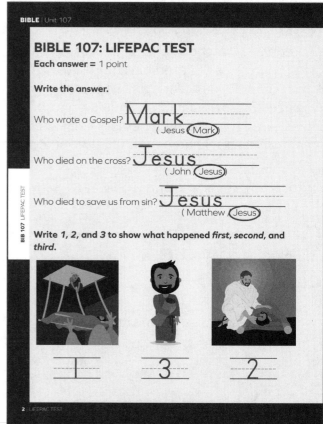

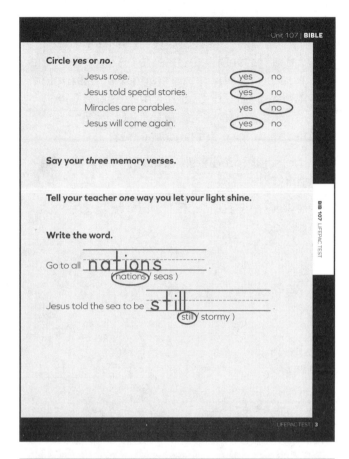

Circle *yes* or *no*.

Jesus rose.   (yes)   no

Jesus told special stories.   (yes)   no

Miracles are parables.   yes   (no)

Jesus will come again.   (yes)   no

Say your *three* memory verses.

Tell your teacher *one* way you let your light shine.

Write the word.

Go to all **nations**
((nations) seas)

Jesus told the sea to be **still**
((still) stormy)

BIB 107 LIFEPAC TEST

LIFEPAC TEST | 3

BIBLE | Unit 107

Draw what happened next.

Jesus stopped the storm.

BIB 107 LIFEPAC TEST

4 | LIFEPAC TEST

ALTERNATE LIFEPAC TEST 107

Administer the test to the class as a group. Ask to have directions read or read them to the class. In either case, be sure that the children clearly understand. Put examples on the board if it seems necessary. Give ample time for each activity to be completed before going to the next.

Correct immediately and discuss with the child.

Review any concepts that have been missed.

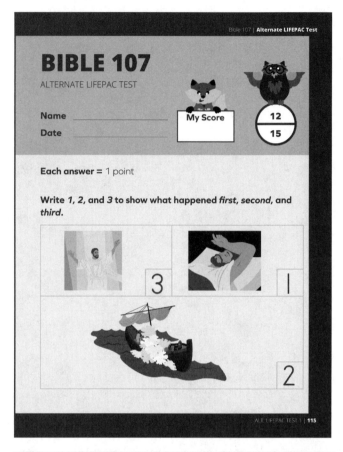

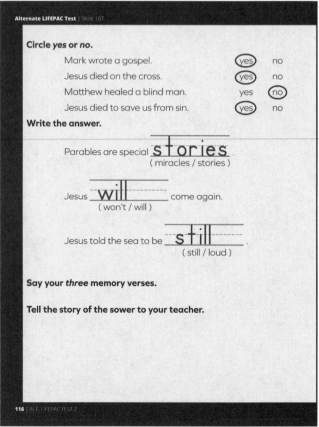

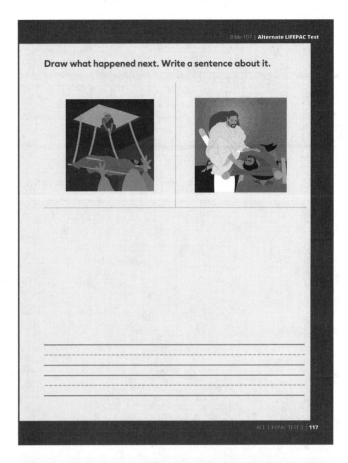

Write the words. Use the words below.

"Let your light _____ before

_____ _____ , that they may see

your _____ _____ , and

_____ your father which

is in _____ .

(Matthew 5:16)

Words to Use

| heaven | men | shine | works | glorify | good |

Bible 107
Worksheet 1
with page 5

✔ Teacher Check _____
Initial   Date

Tell the story.

**Bible 107
Worksheet 2**
with page 9

 ✔ Teacher Check _____

Initial   Date

Follow the dots. Color the pictures. Tell the story.

Teacher Check _____

Initial   Date

Match.

blind ▶   ◀ are raised

lame ▶   ◀ have the gospel preached

lepers ▶   ◀ receive sight

deaf ▶   ◀ are cleansed

dead ▶   ◀ walk

poor ▶   ◀ hear

Bible 107
Worksheet 4
with page 19

Teacher Check _____

                   Initial   Date

Where is Jesus?

Write your answer. Color the picture.

Bible 107
Worksheet 5
with page 29

✔ Teacher Check _____

Initial   Date

BIBLE 107
ALTERNATE LIFEPAC TEST

Name _____

Date _____

My Score

12
15

Each answer = 1 point

Write *1*, *2*, and *3* to show what happened *first*, *second*, and *third*.

Circle *yes* or *no*.

Mark wrote a gospel.	yes	no
Jesus died on the cross.	yes	no
Matthew healed a blind man.	yes	no
Jesus died to save us from sin.	yes	no

Write the answer.

Parables are special _____ .

(miracles / stories)

Jesus _____ come again.

(won't / will)

Jesus told the sea to be _____ .

(still / loud)

Say your *three* memory verses.

Tell the story of the sower to your teacher.

Draw what happened next. Write a sentence about it.

BIBLE 108

Unit 8: God Calls You to Be a Missionary

GOD CALLS YOU TO BE A MISSIONARY
BIBLE 108

Alpha Omega
PUBLICATIONS

804 N. 2nd Ave. E.
Rock Rapids, IA 51246-1759

© MCMXCVI by Alpha Omega Publications, Inc.
All rights reserved.
LIFEPAC is a registered trademark of Alpha Omega Publications, Inc.

Author:
Kathleen McNaughton

Editor:
Mary Ellen Quint, M.A.

Consulting Editor:
John L. Booth, Th.D

Revision Editor:
Alan Christopherson, M.S.

Media Credits:
Page 1: © Askold Romanov, iStock, Thinkstock;
26: ©Tiurin1, iStock, Thinkstock; **28:** © Fanatic Studio, Thinkstock; **32:** © graphic-bee, iStock, Thinkstock.

| i

PAGE 1: GOD CALLS YOU TO BE A MISSIONARY

Concept:

God calls you to be a missionary.

Objective:

To introduce all the objectives.

Teacher Goal:

To introduce this LIFEPAC on being a missionary.

Bible References:

John 3:16; Matthew 28:19

Reading Integration:

Table of contents, main idea

Vocabulary:

missionary, missionaries, woman, (command)
Note: Vocabulary words in parentheses were previously introduced and are being reviewed.

Teaching Page 1:

Pass out the new LIFEPAC. Read the name of the LIFEPAC. Have the children open to the table of contents. Talk about the contents.

What is a contents page for? Into how many sections is the LIFEPAC divided? On what page will you learn about a missionary named Paul? Stephen? What kind of missionaries will you read about in Section 2.

Have the children turn to page 1. Read the page together. Discuss the meaning of the word *missionary*. Bring out the fact that the word *missionary* is never used in the Bible. The Biblical word is *witness*. God calls us to be witnesses for Him. Discuss this word in reference to a witness in a court case. Most children will be somewhat familiar with what happens in a court room.

Reread the page. Substitute the words *witness* for *Jesus* wherever the word *missionary* is printed.

Unit 8 | **GOD CALLS YOU TO BE A MISSIONARY**

GOD CALLS YOU TO BE A MISSIONARY

Missionaries are people who tell others (John 3:16):

"… God so loved the world, that he gave his only begotten Son, that whosoever believeth in him should not perish, but have everlasting life."

When you tell others about Jesus, you are obeying God's command (Matthew 28:19):

"Go ye therefore, and teach all nations …"

Objectives

Read these objectives. They will tell what you will be able to do when you have finished this LIFEPAC®.

1. I can tell about missionaries in the Bible.
2. I can tell about different kinds of missionaries today.
3. I can tell ways that I can be a missionary.

| 1

1. MISSIONARIES IN THE BIBLE

PAGES 2 AND 3

MATERIALS NEEDED

- writing tablet
- Bible
- Worksheet 1

Concept:

Missionaries in the Bible.

Objective:

I can tell about missionaries in the Bible.

Teacher Goals:

To teach the children to name three Bible figures who were missionaries, to say Mark 16:15, and to understand more about what missionaries do.

Bible Reference:

Mark 16:15

Reading Integration:

Main idea, noting and recalling details, following directions, drawing conclusions

Vocabulary:

martyr

Teaching Pages 2 and 3:

Read the title to the children. Introduce the word *martyr*. Talk about what it means. Read page 2 together.

Ask:

"What does the Bible tell us about God's people?"

"What do God's people do?"

"Who are the three people we are going to learn about?"

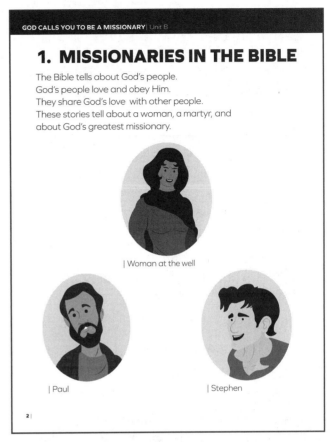

GOD CALLS YOU TO BE A MISSIONARY | Unit 8

1. MISSIONARIES IN THE BIBLE

The Bible tells about God's people.
God's people love and obey Him.
They share God's love with other people.
These stories tell about a woman, a martyr, and about God's greatest missionary.

| Woman at the well

| Paul

| Stephen

2|

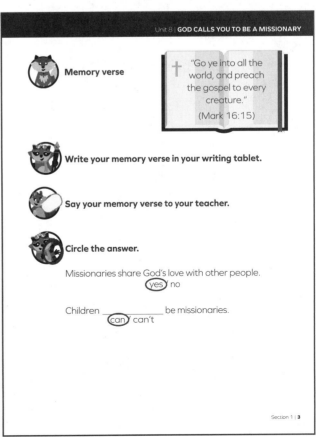

Unit 8 | **GOD CALLS YOU TO BE A MISSIONARY**

Memory verse

"Go ye into all the world, and preach the gospel to every creature."
(Mark 16:15)

Write your memory verse in your writing tablet.

Say your memory verse to your teacher.

Circle the answer.

Missionaries share God's love with other people.
(yes) no

Children _____ be missionaries.
(can) can't

Section 1 | **3**

Tell the children a little about the people in each picture at the top. Review what the word *missionary* means. Tell the children to think of the Christmas story. Ask them to think of some witnesses for Jesus in that story (the angel Gabriel, angels who appeared to the shepherds, the shepherds, the Wise Men).

Read the memory verse from the Bible on page 3. Explain what *Gospel* and *creature* mean. Have the children read it all together from the LIFEPAC. After the children have learned the verse, allow time for them to say it individually.

Complete the activity at the bottom of page 3. Check the sentences as soon as the children are finished.

Activities:

1. Write the memory verse in their writing tablets.

2. Pass out Worksheet 1.

   Review what was said about people in the Christmas story who were missionaries or witnesses for Jesus. When the children have finished, check the page together.

PAGES 4 AND 5: THE WOMAN AT THE WELL

MATERIALS NEEDED

- box screen
- butcher paper
- crayons
- Bible
- pencils
- Worksheet 2

Concept:

The woman at the well.

Objective:

I can tell about missionaries in the Bible.

Teacher Goals:

To teach the children to tell the story of the woman at the well and to tell how she was a missionary.

Bible Reference:

John 4:6–42

Reading Integration:

Main idea, noting and recalling details, following written directions, listening, retelling in own words

Vocabulary:

disciples, believed

Teaching Pages 4 and 5:

Have the open Bible in front of you as you read or tell the story of Jesus and the woman at the well. Have the children open their LIFEPACs to pages 4 and 5. Read the story together.

Ask:

"Why did Jesus and His disciples stop at the well?"

"Where did the disciples go?"

"From whom did Jesus ask a drink?"

"What else did Jesus say to the woman?"

"What did the woman do after she talked to Jesus?"

GOD CALLS YOU TO BE A MISSIONARY | Unit 8

The Woman at the Well
(John 4:6–42)

Jesus and His disciples had walked a long way.
Jesus stopped at a well to rest.
His disciples went to buy food.

A woman came to the well.
Jesus asked her for a drink.

4 | Section 1

Unit 8 | GOD CALLS YOU TO BE A MISSIONARY

Jesus and the woman talked together.
He told her all about her life.
Jesus told her He was
the Savior of the world.

The woman believed Jesus's words.
She went back into the town.
She told the people about Jesus.
Many people from the town
came to listen to Jesus.
They believed in Jesus, too.

● ● ● ● ● ● ● ● ● ● ● ● ● ● ● ● ● ● ●

 Circle the right answer.

Jesus talked to a woman about her life.	(yes)	no
Jesus told her He was the Savior.	(yes)	no
She told other people about Jesus.	(yes)	no

Section 1 | 5

123

"What did she do that shows us she was a missionary, or witness?"

"Did she go to a far away country to be a missionary?"

"Can you be a missionary in your own town, in your neighborhood, or even in your school?"

Read the directions to the activity on page 5. After the children have finished, check the activity together.

Activities:

1. Give several groups of children the opportunity to act out the story of the woman at the well.

2. Make a movie of this story for the box screen. Draw and color the various scenes of the story on a length of butcher paper. Divide the class into small groups of two or three children to work on this project. Each group should draw and color one scene. When all the pictures are finished, attach the paper to the roller. As the pictures are rolled across the screen, several different children should tell the story in parts or as a whole.

3. Pass out Worksheet 2.

Read John 1:40–51 to the children. Who was a missionary in the story? Discuss the picture. What is happening in the picture? Who are the two men? Which one is being a witness, or missionary? Which other disciples in the story were witnesses? Have the children color the picture.

PAGES 6 AND 7: STEPHEN, GOD'S MARTYR

MATERIALS NEEDED

- pencils
- writing tablet

Concept:

Stephen, the first martyr.

Objective:

I can tell about missionaries in the Bible.

Teacher Goal:

To teach the story of Stephen's faith.

Bible Reference:

Acts 6:1–8:3

Reading Integration:

Main idea, noting and recalling details, following written directions

Vocabulary:

Stephen, (martyr)
Note: Vocabulary words in parentheses were previously introduced and are being reviewed.

Teaching Pages 6 and 7:

Write *Stephen* and *martyr* on the board. Say the words but do not explain *martyr*. Tell the children to watch for the word in the story to find out what it means.

Have the children open their books to pages 6 and 7 and read the story to themselves. Talk about it.

Ask:

"What are the two things Stephen did that some people did not like?"

"What did these people do to Stephen?"

"Why was Stephen killed?"

"What did Stephen do for the men who killed him?"

"What is a martyr?"

Read the directions on page 7. Check the activity as soon as the children are finished.

GOD CALLS YOU TO BE A MISSIONARY | Unit 8

Stephen, God's Martyr
(Acts 6–8)

Stephen was a man of God.
Stephen believed in Jesus.
Stephen told others about Jesus.
Stephen worked miracles.

Some men did not like what Stephen said.
They spoke against him.
They had people lie about him.

| Stephen

6 | Section 1

Unit 8 | GOD CALLS YOU TO BE A MISSIONARY

Finally, they decided
that Stephen must die.
They killed Stephen with stones
because he believed in Jesus
and told others about Him.
Stephen forgave the men who killed him.
Stephen was the first martyr.
A martyr dies for his faith.

● ● ● ● ● ● ● ● ● ● ● ● ● ● ● ● ● ● ● ●

Write the word.

Stephen was a ___martyr___ .
(martyr / faith)

Stephen told others about ___Jesus___
(Jesus / Paul)

Stephen worked ___miracles___
(days / miracles)

Section 1 | 7

Activities:

1. Have the children write a prayer in their writing tablets asking God to make them brave witnesses for Jesus and able to always show love to other people, even their enemies.

2. Review the memory verse, Mark 16:15.

PAGES 8 AND 9: PAUL, GOD'S SERVANT

MATERIALS NEEDED

- writing tablet
- drawing paper
- crayons
- pencils
- map of the ancient Roman empire or current world map

Concept:

Paul, a servant of Jesus Christ.

Objective:

I can tell about missionaries in the Bible.

Teacher Goals:

To teach the children to tell what it means to be a servant of Jesus Christ, to tell about Paul, the missionary, and to see themselves as servants of Jesus, just like Paul.

Bible Reference:

Acts 9–28

Reading Integration:

Main idea, noting and recalling details, following written directions, writing a story, speaking in a group, listening

GOD CALLS YOU TO BE A MISSIONARY | Unit 8

Paul, God's Servant

A servant is a person who works for someone else.
Missionaries are God's servants.
They obey God's command to tell the world about Jesus.
Paul was God's greatest missionary.
God tells us many things about Paul in the Bible.
We know that Paul went to many cities and countries.

8 | Section 1

Vocabulary:

Paul, cities, countries, Christians, promises, (important, servant)
Note: Vocabulary words in parentheses were previously introduced and are being reviewed.

Teaching Pages 8 and 9:

Introduce the story of Paul by telling briefly of his conversion experience. Explain that he had hated Christians and did everything he could to get rid of them. Then Jesus Himself appeared to Paul and he became a believer. At first, it was hard for other Christians to believe Paul had changed. But he showed so much love for people and for Jesus that other Christians finally accepted him and were not afraid of him any longer.

Have the children open their LIFEPACs to pages 8 and 9 while you print the vocabulary words on the board.

Read through the words several times together.

Read pages 8 and 9 together, discussing as you read them. On the map, show the children the places where Paul traveled.

After reading the two pages, use the activity on page 9 as a group project.

Activities:

1. Review and say John 3:16 and Mark 16:15 together or individually.

2. Read some of the stories about Paul from a Bible story book.

Everywhere Paul went,
he told people about God's love.
He told them that Jesus
died on the cross for their sins.
This news made many people sad.
Then Paul would tell them
that Jesus rose again
on the third day.
Because Jesus rose again,
Christians will go to heaven.
They will live with Jesus in heaven forever.
This news made the people happy again.

Many people believed in Jesus
because Paul obeyed God.
Every day, Paul asked God
for help to do this important job.

God wants you to be a missionary, too.
He promises to help you,
just like He helped Paul.

● ● ● ● ● ● ● ● ● ● ● ● ● ● ● ● ● ● ● ●

 Discuss everything Paul told people about God's love.

Section 1 | **9**

PAGE 10: ACTIVITY PAGE

MATERIALS NEEDED

- pencils
- flannel board

Teaching Page 10:

Review the vocabulary and stories from Section 1. Use flashcards or word chart. Story review may be accomplished through retelling the stories by the children or teacher, possibly using the flannel board. Teaching pictures and questions may be used.

Then read all the directions and identify any illustrations. Allow the children enough time to finish page 10 before checking it together. Page 10 should be checked before going on to the Self Test.

The students should prepare for the Self Test. Ask the students to look over and read the Self Test but they should not write the answers to any questions. After looking over the Self Test the students should go to the beginning of the unit and reread the text and review the answers to the activities up to the Self Test.

The students are to complete the Self Test the next school day. This should be done under regular test conditions without allowing the students to look back. A good idea is to clip the pages together before the test.

GOD CALLS YOU TO BE A MISSIONARY | Unit 8

Match the pictures and words.

martyr

well

servant

Circle the right word.

Stephen _____ a good man.
((was) wasn't)

Jesus _____ our Savior.
(isn't (is))

God's people _____ share God's love.
(will (won't))

You _____ be a missionary.
(can (can't))

Before you take the Self Test, study what you have read and done. The Self Test will check what you remember.

10 | Section 1

PAGE 11: SELF TEST 1

MATERIALS NEEDED

• pencils

Concept:

Evaluation.

Objective:

I can tell about missionaries in the Bible.

Teacher Goal:

To evaluate the children's progress.

Bible References:

Review memory verse and all other Bible references.

Reading Integration:

Following written directions, recalling details, contractions

Vocabulary:

Review all vocabulary words.

Teaching Page 11:

Have the children turn to page 11 in their LIFEPACs. Read the directions together. Answer any questions about what to do. Allow the children sufficient time to complete the page. Check the page as soon as possible after all are finished.

Listen to the memory verse individually.

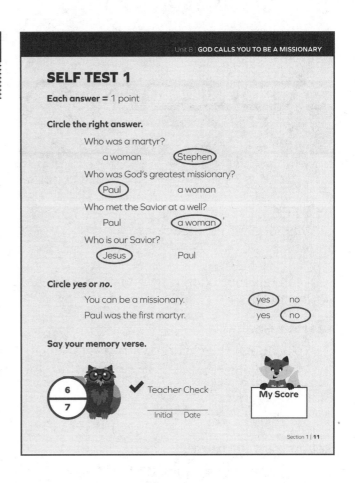

Unit 8 | **GOD CALLS YOU TO BE A MISSIONARY**

SELF TEST 1

Each answer = 1 point

Circle the right answer.

Who was a martyr?

a woman   (Stephen)

Who was God's greatest missionary?

(Paul)   a woman

Who met the Savior at a well?

Paul   (a woman)

Who is our Savior?

(Jesus)   Paul

Circle yes or no.

You can be a missionary.   (yes)   no

Paul was the first martyr.   yes   (no)

Say your memory verse.

6 / 7

✔ Teacher Check

Initial   Date

My Score

Section 1 | **11**

2. MISSIONARIES TODAY
PAGES 12 AND 13

MATERIALS NEEDED

- crayons
- pencils
- writing tablet

Concept:

Missionaries of today.

Objective:

I can tell about different kinds of missionaries today.

Teacher Goal:

To acquaint the children with several kinds of missionaries.

Bible Reference:

Matthew 28:19

Reading Integration:

Main idea, noting and recalling details, drawing conclusions

Vocabulary:

radio, nations, (pilots, auto repairmen)
Note: Vocabulary words in parentheses were previously introduced and are being reviewed.

Teaching Pages 12 and 13:

Talk about the pictures on pages 12 and 13. Ask the children to tell what they think the man on page 12 is telling the people. Have the children find the church in the picture and put a circle around it. Have them tell why they think it is a church.

Read page 12 together. Talk about it. Have the children underline the kinds of jobs missionaries do.

Things to talk about:

"How can a pilot serve as a witness or missionary to Jesus?"

"Why would an auto repairman be an important missionary?"

"What are some other jobs missionaries might do?"

Tell the children to color the picture on page 13.

---

2. MISSIONARIES TODAY

God's missionaries travel
to many places in the world.
Some countries do not allow
missionaries to come.
The people in those countries learn of Jesus
from the radio, television, or the Internet.
Many missionaries are pastors.
Some are doctors and nurses.
Others are teachers, pilots,
and auto repairmen.
All are helping to tell
of God's love in all nations.

12 | Section 2

Activities:

1. Write stories about the missionary in the picture on page 13. Tell what he is saying.

2. Invite a missionary who is home on furlough to come and talk to the children. Prepare questions that the children would like answered.

PAGES 14 AND 15: PASTOR MISSIONARIES

MATERIALS NEEDED

- Bible
- pencils
- books about missionaries

Concept:

Missionaries who serve as pastors.

Objective:

I can tell about different kinds of missionaries today.

Teacher Goal:

To help the children gain a realistic idea of what missionary pastors do.

Bible References:

Mark 16:15; Matthew 28:19

Reading Integration:

Main idea, noting and recalling details, following directions, drawing conclusions

Vocabulary:

language, pastors

Teaching Pages 14 and 15:

Ask the children to list some things they think a person would have to know to be a good witness or missionary for Jesus in another country.

Write *pastors* and *language* on the board. Read the words to the class. Ask the children why the pastor should learn the language. Can the children think of any way they could tell about God's love without knowing the other person's language?

Read page 14 together. Discuss the page. Why do people need missionaries? What does the pastor do first when in a new country? To whom does the pastor tell God's Good News? What is the Good News? (Say John 3:16 together.)

GOD CALLS YOU TO BE A MISSIONARY | Unit 8

Pastor Missionaries

God calls many pastors to be
His missionaries.
In many countries, people
have never heard of Jesus.
They do not know that Jesus died for them.
They do not know that God loves them.
Pastor missionaries first learn
the language of the people.
Then they tell the Good News
of God's love to all who will listen.

14 | Section 2

Unit 8 | GOD CALLS YOU TO BE A MISSIONARY

Find the answer in the story.
Write the answer.

Who calls pastors to be missionaries?

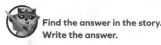
God

What do missionaries have to learn?

language of the people

What do missionaries tell people?

Good News of God's Love

Memory verse

"Go ye therefore, and teach all nations, baptizing them in the name of the Father, and of the Son, and of the Holy Ghost."
(Matthew 28:19)

Section 2 | 15

Read the memory verse on page 15. What does the pastor do after he teaches the people about salvation?

Have the children read this verse together several times. Assign it to be learned. Read the directions at the top of the page. Encourage the children to be careful with their spelling as they copy the answer to the questions

Activity:

Read or tell stories of modern missionaries in foreign countries or here at home in the United States. Many mission fields are here in our country that the children should be aware of.

PAGES 16 AND 17: MEDICAL MISSIONARIES

MATERIALS NEEDED

- drawing paper
- writting tablet
- flannel board
- construction paper
- tongue depressors

Concept:

Medical missionaries.

Objective:

I can tell about different kinds of missionaries today.

Teacher Goal:

To teach the children about missionaries who are in the medical profession.

Bible References:

Luke 6:31, Matthew 25:40

Reading Integration:

Main idea, noting and recalling details, writing sentences

Vocabulary:

hungry, medical

Teaching Pages 16 and 17:

Write *hungry* and *medical* on the board. Talk about the meaning of *medical*. Read page 16 together. Talk about the pictures on pages 16 and 17. Discuss the story.

Who calls doctors and nurses to be missionaries? Why are medical missionaries important? What do medical missionaries do? What are the people in the picture on page 17 doing?

Read the Bible verses on page 17 in unison and talk about what they mean. Discuss the different ways that Christians here in America can help the needy in other countries without going there.

GOD CALLS YOU TO BE A MISSIONARY | Unit 8

Medical Missionaries

God calls doctors and nurses
to be His missionaries.
Many people in the world
are sick and hungry.
God sends doctors and nurses
to help them.

The doctors and nurses
teach the people that God loves them
and cares for them.
These doctors and nurses
are medical missionaries.

16 | Section 2

Unit 8 | GOD CALLS YOU TO BE A MISSIONARY

 **Learn the Golden Rule.**

"And as ye would that men should do to you, do ye also to them likewise."

(Luke 6:31)

Jesus tells us (Matthew 25:40):
"… Inasmuch as ye have done it unto one of the least of these my brethren, ye have done it unto me."

Section 2 | 17

Activities:

1. Have the children draw a picture of something they can do here at home to help missionaries in foreign lands.

2. Write prayers asking God to bless the work of all Christian missionaries.

3. Retell the story of the Good Samaritan and talk about how the Samaritan acted as a missionary. Flannel board figures or puppets might be used to tell the story. Stick puppets can easily be made from construction paper and tongue depressors.

PAGES 18 AND 19: BIBLE TRANSLATORS

MATERIALS NEEDED

- crayons
- pencils
- Bible or portion of a Bible in another language
- Worksheet 3

Concept:

Bible translators.

Objective:

I can tell about different kinds of missionaries today.

Teacher Goal:

To acquaint the children with the work of Bible translators.

Bible References:

Mark 16:15; Matthew 28:19

Reading Integration:

Left to right, listening, speaking in a group, small group discussion, oral and written directions

Vocabulary:

translators, (special)
Note: Vocabulary words in parentheses were previously introduced and are being reviewed.

Teaching Pages 18 and 19:

Hand the foreign Bible to one of the children and ask them to read a verse. Talk about what it would be like to have only Bibles in foreign languages from which to read and learn. Ask how the children would feel if no books at all were in English.

How would you learn about Jesus if there were no Bible to read from? How would you learn anything if there were no books in English?

Bible Translators

Many people in the world
have no Bible to read.
The Bible has never been written
in their languages.
God calls some missionaries
to help these people.
They have the special job of writing
the Bible in new languages.
They are called *translators*.
They also teach the people
how to read their languages.
How joyful the people are
to read about God's love.

18 | Section 2

Unit 8 | **GOD CALLS YOU TO BE A MISSIONARY**

Circle *yes* or *no*.

Only pastors can be missionaries.	yes (no)
Some missionaries are doctors.	(yes) no
A translator writes down the Bible in new languages.	(yes) no

Draw the face of a person who has just learned to read the Bible.

Section 2 | **19**

In some countries, the language has never been written down. No books at all are in that country for the people to read in their own language. All learning is only by hearing. Have the children open their LIFEPACs to page 18. Read the page together. Discuss the work of Bible translators. Explain that these missionaries must live in the foreign countries a long time to learn how best to speak and write the language of the people in that country. It takes many years to finish writing the Bible in a whole new language.

Have the children complete the activities on page 19.

Activity:

Pass out Worksheet 3.

Instruct the student(s) on how to complete the dot-to-dot activity. Explain that this boy is a Navajo Indian who lives in the United States. In 1965, the first copy of a New Testament in the Navajo language was printed. For the very first time that year, Navajo people could read the Good News of God's love for themselves in their own language. The words on the cover of the book in the picture say "God's Word." If any American Indian people are living in your area, perhaps a copy of a Bible in their language could be obtained. An American Indian pastor or evangelist might be invited to visit the class and talk about the work he does among his own people.

The Bible has been translated into many languages.

GOD BIZAAD

Bible 108
Worksheet 3
with page 19

Teacher Check _____
Initial   Date

157

PAGES 20 AND 21: RADIO MISSIONARIES

MATERIALS NEEDED

- pencils
- crayons
- writing tablet
- word cards
- word chart

Concept:

Radio missionaries.

Objective:

I can tell about different kinds of missionaries today.

Teacher Goals:

To acquaint the children with radio ministries and to help the children learn something of the persecuted church today.

Bible References:

Mark 16:15, Matthew 28:19

Reading Integration:

Main idea, noting and recalling details, following written directions

Vocabulary:

allowed, reaches, (radio)
Note: Vocabulary words in parentheses were previously introduced and are being reviewed.

Teaching Pages 20 and 21:

Ask the children to describe the picture on page 20. Tell them that families are listening to God's Word. It might be the only way they can hear about Jesus. Their government does not allow them to have Bibles or to go to church. In some countries, they could be punished for listening to God's Word on the radio.

Read the page together and talk about it. Lead the children to a real appreciation and an attitude of thankfulness to God for the freedom they have to worship together, to go to a Christian school and church, and to own a Bible.

Review the different kinds of missionaries the children have learned about. Read the directions on page 21 together. Check the activity after the children have completed it.

Activities:

1. Write a prayer in the writing tablet, asking God to protect Christians who live under the threat of persecution.

2. As a class, write a radio program for people who have no churches or Bibles. Include music in the program. Give the program for other classes in the school or as a presentation to parents.

3. Review the vocabulary words from Sections 1 and 2. Use flashcards or a word chart.

4. Review both memory verses.

The students should prepare for the Self Test. Ask the students to look over and read the Self Test but they should not write the answers to any questions. After looking over the Self Test the students should go to the beginning of the unit and reread the text and review the answers to the activities up to the Self Test.

The students are to complete the Self Test the next school day. This should be done under regular test conditions without allowing the students to look back. A good idea is to clip the pages together before the test.

PAGE 22: SELF TEST 2

MATERIALS NEEDED

- glue
- scissors
- pencils
- magazines
- tongue depressors
- *Make-it-yourself Pattern Encyclopedia* or online templates

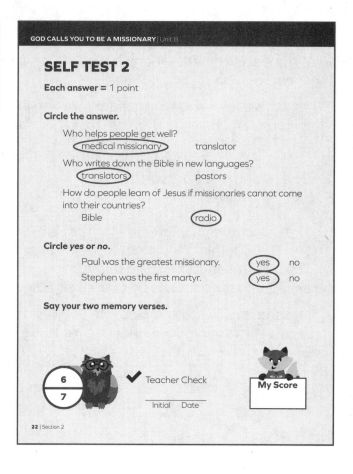

GOD CALLS YOU TO BE A MISSIONARY| Unit 8

SELF TEST 2

Each answer = 1 point

Circle the answer.

Who helps people get well?
(medical missionary)   translator

Who writes down the Bible in new languages?
(translators)   pastors

How do people learn of Jesus if missionaries cannot come into their countries?
Bible   (radio)

Circle *yes* or *no*.

Paul was the greatest missionary.   (yes)   no

Stephen was the first martyr.   (yes)   no

Say your *two* memory verses.

6/7   ✔ Teacher Check

_____ _____
Initial   Date

My Score

22 | Section 2

Concept:

Missionaries today.

Objectives:

I can tell about missionaries in the Bible.

I can tell about different kinds of missionaries today.

Teacher Goal:

To evaluate the children's progress.

Bible References:

Matthew 28:19; Mark 16:15; Luke 6:31; Matthew 25:40

Reading Integration:

Recalling details, following written directions.

Vocabulary:

Review all vocabulary words.

Teaching Page 22:

Have the children turn to page 22 in their LIFEPACs. Read the directions together. Answer any questions about what to do. Allow the children sufficient time to complete the page. Check the page as soon as possible after all are finished. Listen to the memory verses individually as the children complete the test.

Activity:

Make stick puppets of children of many nations. Use patterns such as those in the *Pattern Encyclopedia* or online templates, or cut pictures of children from magazines. Mount the pictures on cardboard and glue a tongue depressor to the back of each one. Use the puppets to put on plays about mission work in foreign lands and here at home.

3. MISSIONARIES GOD CALLS

PAGE 23

Unit 8 | **GOD CALLS YOU TO BE A MISSIONARY**

3. MISSIONARIES GOD CALLS

God calls His children to be missionaries for Him.
In the Bible, God says:
"Ye are the light of the world."
You are God's light when you
share His love with others.
Your light can shine in your home,
at school, and in your neighborhood.

Section 3 | **23**

MATERIALS NEEDED

- writing tablet
- lamp without a shade
- pail
- large box or large grocery sack
- crayons
- Worksheet 4

Concept:

God calls missionaries.

Objective:

I can tell ways I can be a missionary.

Teacher Goal:

To impress on the children that God calls all His people to be His witnesses.

Bible References:

Matthew 28:19; Matthew 5:16; James 1:22

Reading Integration:

Main idea, noting and recalling details, predicting outcomes, sequence

Vocabulary:

neighborhood

Teaching Page 23:

Tell the children to close their eyes or take the class to a very dark room.

Ask:
    "How much can you see and learn when everything is dark?"

Turn on the lights or open eyes.

Ask them:
    "Now can you see and learn?"

Christians are like this light. The people of the world are like people in a dark room. They cannot find their way around. They cannot find their way to heaven. But then a Christian comes on the scene and immediately lights up the dark world. By words and actions, a Christian shows people the way to heaven. God tells Christians that they are the light of the world.

Read page 23 together. Talk about ways to let God's light shine in the world around you.

Activity:

Pass out Worksheet 4.

Talk about what is happening in each picture. Tell the children to show what they would do next in each situation.

PAGES 24 AND 25: AT HOME

MATERIALS NEEDED

- Bible
- crayons
- pencils
- writing tablet

Concept:

Being a witness at home.

Objective:

I can tell ways that I can be a missionary.

Teacher Goal:

To help the children explore ways they can be helpful at home.

Bible References:

Matthew 5:16; Ephesians 6:1–3; Colossians 3:20 and 23

Reading Integration:

Main idea, noting and recalling details, speaking in a group, listening

GOD CALLS YOU TO BE A MISSIONARY | Unit 8

In Your Home

Being a missionary at home
helps make home a happy place.
Remember, a missionary shares
God's love with others.
You can share God's love
by the way you act.
When you obey your parents
or help your brother or sister,
you are sharing God's love.

Think of other ways to share
God's love at home.

24 | Section 3

Teaching Pages 24 and 25:

Review the meaning of the word *missionary* (a witness). Let the children explain what it means to be a witness to Jesus.

Read page 24 together. Read Ephesians 6:1–3, Colossians 3:20 and 23 to the children. Talk about what these verses mean, especially the last one. Ask the children how they think they would act toward Jesus if He lived in their homes as a real human person that they could see. Point out that is how Colossians 3:23 is saying we should act toward all people.

List on the board as many ways as the children can think of to be witnesses at home.

Have the children draw their pictures on page 25. These pictures should be personal resolutions. Allow those children who wish to share their picture the opportunity to do so.

Activity:

Have the children write a prayer in their writing tablets thanking God for their families and asking His help in carrying out the resolutions they made to let their lights shine at home.

Unit 8 | **GOD CALLS YOU TO BE A MISSIONARY**

Draw a picture of one way you can share God's love at home.

Talk about your picture.

Section 3 | **25**

PAGES 26 AND 27: IN YOUR NEIGHBORHOOD

MATERIALS NEEDED

- pencils

Concept:

You are called to be a witness in your neighborhood.

Objective:

I can tell ways that I can be a missionary.

Teacher Goal:

To inspire the children to be witnesses in their neighborhoods.

Bible References:

Matthew 5:16; James 1:22

Reading Integration:

Main idea, noting idea, noting and recalling details, following written directions

Vocabulary:

litter, neighbors, (neighborhood)
Note: Vocabulary words in parentheses were previously introduced and are being reviewed.

Teaching Pages 26 and 27:

Write the vocabulary words on the board. Read the words to the class. Tell the children to think about some of the people who live close to them in their neighborhoods.

Ask them:

"Do any old people who live there need help doing things around their houses?"

"Are there many children?"

"Are they younger, the same age, or older?"

"Is there ever litter lying around in the neighborhood?"

GOD CALLS YOU TO BE A MISSIONARY | Unit 8

In Your Neighborhood

Think about the neighbors who live around you.
How can you share God's love with them?
Is there someone who needs your help?
Do you have a friend you can tell about Jesus?
Is litter lying around that you could help clean up?

One thing Jesus tells you to do is "let your light shine."
Think of more ways to let your light shine
in your neighborhood.

26 | Section 3

Unit 8 | GOD CALLS YOU TO BE A MISSIONARY

Memory verse

"But be ye doers of the word, and not hearers only."
(James 1:22)

Circle the children who are letting their lights shine.

Section 3 | 27

Open the LIFEPACs to page 26 and read about being a witness in your neighborhood. List all the ways the children can think of that they might let their lights shine out to the people who live around them.

Learn the memory verse on page 27. Say it together several times. Talk about what it means. When the children let their lights shine in their neighborhoods and at home, they are being doers of the Word.

Complete and check the activity at the bottom of page 27.

PAGES 28 AND 29: AT SCHOOL

MATERIALS NEEDED

- crayons
- Bible
- writing tablet

Concept:

You are called to witness at school.

Objective:

I can tell ways that I can be a missionary.

Teacher Goal:

To teach the children how to witness to peers and others at school.

Bible References:

James 1:22; Matthew 5:16

Reading Integration:

Main idea, noting and recalling details, following written directions, speaking in a group, listening

Vocabulary:

respect, classmates, forgiveness

GOD CALLS YOU TO BE A MISSIONARY | Unit 8

At School

Let your light shine in your classroom.
Respect and obey your teachers.
Be kind and helpful to your classmates.
You can share God's love and forgiveness
wherever you are and
whatever you are doing.
You cannot do it by yourself.
Every day, ask God for His help.
He promises to hear you and
to answer your prayer.

28 | Section 3

Teaching Pages 28 and 29:

Read Matthew 5:16 from the Bible to the class. Talk about what it means.

"How do you let your light shine?" (doing good works)

"Why do you do good things?" (so people will glorify God)

"What does glorify mean?" (to praise)

"How can you let your light shine at school?"

Read page 28 together. Have the children underline all the things they can do at school to let their lights shine. List any others they think of on the board.

Have each child decide on one thing they are going to do with God's help that they have not done before. Tell them to draw a picture of what they are going to do on page 29. Allow time for those who want to share their pictures to do so.

Activity:

Have the children write about several things in their writing tablets that they can do at school to let their lights shine in the classroom.

PAGES 30 AND 31: ACTIVITY PAGES

MATERIALS NEEDED

- crayons
- writing tablets
- word cards
- word chart

Teaching Pages 30 and 31:

Read the memory verse on page 30 all together several times. Review what it means.

After the children have drawn their pictures, share some of the ideas presented with the whole class.

Read the directions on page 31. After the children are finished, talk about the two pictures. Find out how the children feel about what is happening in the first picture. Ask what they would do if they saw something like that happening.

Activities:

1. Have each child write a letter to their parents explaining the project they want to undertake in their neighborhood or in their home.

2. A week or two later, have the children write a follow-up story. In it they should tell how their project is progressing or how it has worked out.

3. Review the contents of this LIFEPAC. Check the children's recall of the stories in Section 1 and the kinds of modern day missionaries in Section 2. Review the four memory verses and all the vocabulary words.

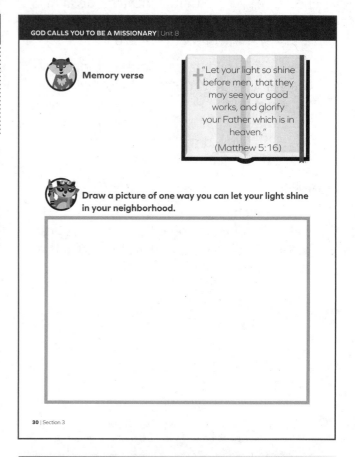

GOD CALLS YOU TO BE A MISSIONARY | Unit 8

Memory verse

"Let your light so shine before men, that they may see your good works, and glorify your Father which is in heaven."
(Matthew 5:16)

Draw a picture of one way you can let your light shine in your neighborhood.

30 | Section 3

Unit 8 | GOD CALLS YOU TO BE A MISSIONARY

Color the picture of children being good missionaries.

Section 3 | 31

PAGE 32: ACTIVITY PAGE

MATERIALS NEEDED

- pencils
- Worksheet 5

Teaching Page 32:

Read the directions on page 32. Instruct the children that they are to draw lines from the picture to the right word. Remind them to answer the question at the bottom of the page. Check together and discuss as a review.

Activities:

1. Review the entire LIFEPAC, concentrating on any areas that may have caused difficulties on the self tests.

2. Pass out Worksheet 5.

   Have the children fill in the blanks with the words in the boxes.

The students should prepare for the Self Test. Ask the students to look over and read the Self Test but they should not write the answers to any questions. After looking over the Self Test the students should go to the beginning of the unit and reread the text and review the answers to the activities up to the Self Test.

The students are to complete the Self Test the next school day. This should be done under regular test conditions without allowing the students to look back. A good idea is to clip the pages together before the test.

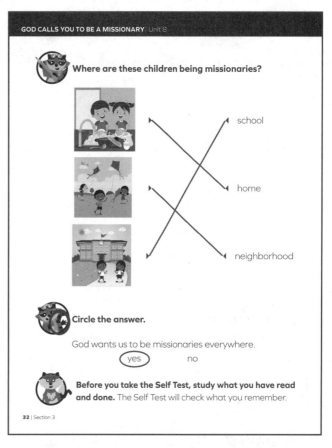

PAGE 33: SELF TEST 3

MATERIALS NEEDED

• pencils

Concept:

Evaluation.

Objectives:

I can tell about missionaries in the Bible.

I can tell about different kinds of missionaries today.

I can tell ways that I can be a missionary.

Teacher Goal:

To evaluate the children's work.

Bible References:

Review all Bible references and memory verses.

Vocabulary:

Review all vocabulary words.

Teaching Page 33:

Have the children turn to page 33 in their LIFEPACs. Read the directions together. Answer any questions about what to do. Identify all illustrations. Allow the children sufficient time to complete the page. Check the page as soon as all are finished. Listen to the memory verses individually as the children complete the test.

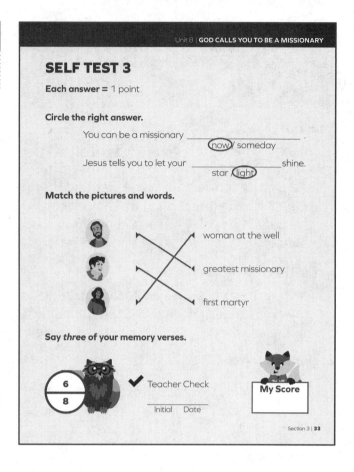

LIFEPAC TEST 108

Administer the test to the class as a group. Ask to have directions read or read them to the class. In either case, be sure that the children clearly understand. Put examples on the board if it seems necessary. Give ample time for each activity to be completed before going to the next.

Correct immediately and discuss with the child.

Review any concepts that have been missed.

Give those children who do not achieve the 80% score additional copies of the worksheets and a list of vocabulary words to study. A parent or a classroom helper should help in the review.

When the child is ready, give the Alternate LIFEPAC Test. Use the same procedure as for the LIFEPAC Test.

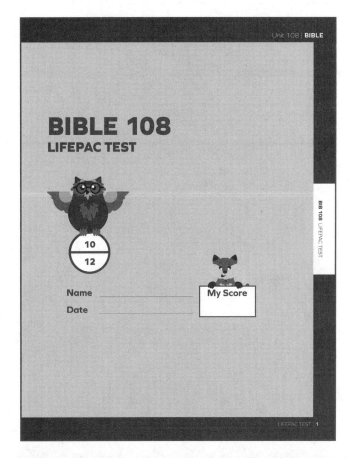

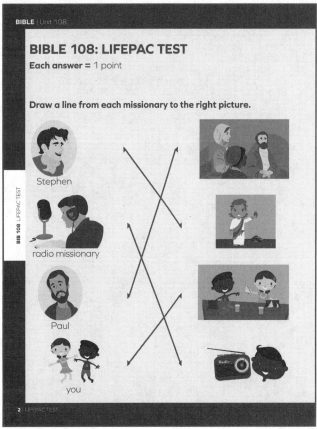

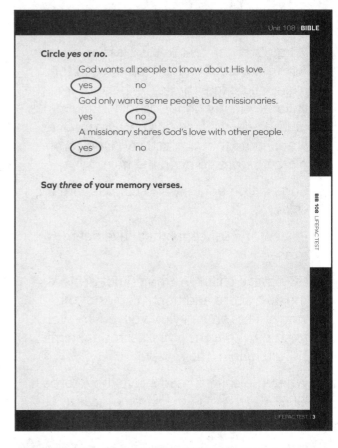

ALTERNATE LIFEPAC TEST 108

Administer the test to the class as a group. Ask to have directions read or read them to the class. In either case, be sure that the children clearly understand. Put examples on the board if it seems necessary. Give ample time for each activity to be completed before going to the next.

Correct immediately and discuss with the child.

Review any concepts that have been missed.

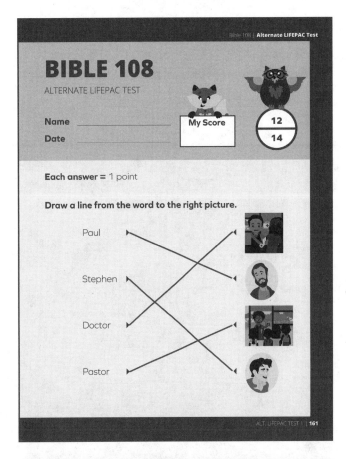

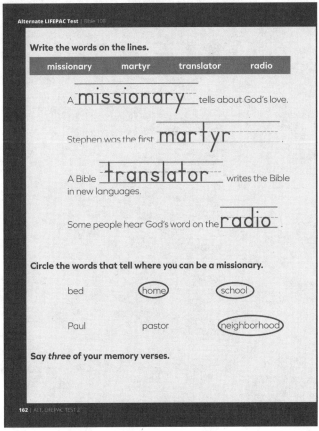

_____

Circle the witnesses for Jesus's birth.

**Bible 108
Worksheet 1**
with page 3

✔ Teacher Check _____

Initial   Date

Andrew shared his faith with his brother, Simon Peter.

"We have found the Messiah."

Bible 108
Worksheet 2
with page 5

Teacher Check _____
Initial   Date

The Bible has been translated into many languages.

GOD
BIZAAD

**Bible 108
Worksheet 3**
with page 19

✓ Teacher Check _____
Initial   Date

Draw and tell what you would do next.

**Bible 108
Worksheet 4**
with page 23

✔ Teacher Check _____
                  Initial   Date

Memory Verse Review

Gospel   creature world

"Go ye into all the _____

and preach the _____

to every _____ .

(Mark 16:15)

heaven   glorify   light   good

"Let your _____ so shine before men,

that they may see your _____ works, and

_____ your father which is in

_____ "

_____ .

(Matthew 5:16)

**Bible 108
Worksheet 5**
with page 32

✔ Teacher Check _____
Initial   Date

BIBLE 108

ALTERNATE LIFEPAC TEST

Name _____

Date _____

My Score

12
14

Each answer = 1 point

Draw a line from the word to the right picture.

Paul ▶ ◀

Stephen ▶ ◀

Doctor ▶ ◀

Pastor ▶ ◀

Write the words on the lines.

missionary	martyr	translator	radio

A _____ tells about God's love.

Stephen was the first _____ .

A Bible _____ writes the Bible in new languages.

Some people hear God's word on the _____ .

Circle the words that tell where you can be a missionary.

bed   home   school

Paul   pastor   neighborhood

Say *three* of your memory verses.

BIBLE 109

Unit 9: New Testament Stories

NEW TESTAMENT STORIES
BIBLE 109

Alpha Omega
PUBLICATIONS

804 N. 2nd Ave. E.
Rock Rapids, IA 51246-1759

Author:
Pam Slagter, B.A.

Managing Editor:
Alan Christopherson, M.S.

Layout/Editorial:
Carrie Rice, B.S., Jennifer Davis, B.S.

Media Credits:
Page 1: © Annasunny, iStock, Thinkstock.

|i

PAGE 1: NEW TESTAMENT STORIES

MATERIALS NEEDED

- pencils
- brown construction paper
- lined penmanship paper

Concepts:

The Bible is divided into the Old and New Testaments. The New Testament was written after Jesus was born. We can read and learn about men, women, and children in the New Testament.

Objective:

Students will read that God took care of men, women, and children in the New Testament.

Teacher Goal:

Review what the word *testament* means and tell the students that they will read about some men, women, and children from the New Testament.

Vocabulary:

Review the word *testament* from Unit 5.

Teaching Page 1:

1. Remind the students that the Bible is God's word. It was written many years ago, and we can learn about God from stories in the Bible.

2. Read the top part of page 1 with the students. Explain to them that the Bible is divided into two parts. These parts are called the Old Testament and the New Testament. Review with them what the word *testament* means (from page 1 of Unit 5).

3. Read the objectives with the students. Tell the students to circle the words that are different in each objective sentence (*stories*, *men*, *women*, and *children*). Tell them that they will read about these groups of people in this unit.

Activity:

Make a New Testament booklet by folding the construction paper in half for the cover of the booklet. Write "New Testament" on the cover. Fold the lined penmanship paper in half. Write on the first page:

> **The New Testament was written after Jesus was born.**
>
> **I can learn about God from these stories.**

Save these booklets since the students will be writing in them throughout the unit. (This activity is similar to the activity of Unit 5, page 1 of the Old Testament LIFEPAC).

1. MEN OF THE NEW TESTAMENT

PAGE 2: LAZARUS

Concepts:

Lazarus, Thomas, and Stephen are men in the New Testament. Lazarus was a friend of Jesus who became very sick.

Objectives:

Students will know some stories from the New Testament.

Students will know some men of the New Testament.

Teacher Goals:

To teach the children to name Lazarus, Thomas, and Stephen as men from the New Testament and be able to describe their stories and to have them read and remember that Lazarus had two sisters and was a friend of Jesus.

Bible Reference:

John 11:1–44

Vocabulary:

Lazarus, Thomas, Stephen, sister, brother, sick

Teaching Page 2:

1. Tell the students that they will be learning about three men from the New Testament. Read the top of page 2 together.

2. Tell the students that they are going to read about Lazarus. Read the rest of page 2 together.

NEW TESTAMENT STORIES | Unit 9

1. MEN OF THE NEW TESTAMENT

You will learn about Lazarus.
You will learn about Thomas.
You will learn about Stephen.
You will learn how God helped these men.

Lazarus
(John 11:1–44)

Mary and Martha were sisters.
Lazarus was their brother.
They were friends of Jesus.
Jesus would stay at their home.
They loved Jesus.
One day, Lazarus became very sick.
Mary and Martha were worried!
Jesus was in another town.

| Lazarus

2 | Section 1

PAGE 3: LAZARUS

MATERIALS NEEDED

- pencils
- crayons
- Worksheet 1

Concepts:

Lazarus was a good friend of Jesus. Lazarus became very sick and died. Jesus wept when he heard that Lazarus was dead. Jesus performed a miracle and made Lazarus alive again.

Objectives:

Students will know some stories from the New Testament.

Students will know some men of the New Testament.

Teacher Goal:

Read together the continuing story of Lazarus.

Bible Reference:

John 11:1–44

Vocabulary:

heal, wept, alive

Teaching Page 3:

1. Review that Lazarus was a good friend of Jesus. Ask the students if they can remember the names of Lazarus's sisters (Mary & Martha).

2. Read page 3 together. Discuss the illustration on page 3.

Activity:

Look at Worksheet 1 with the students. Point out to them that only one half of the butterfly is drawn. They are to make other half like the drawn part. Tell them to color the two parts of the butterfly the same.

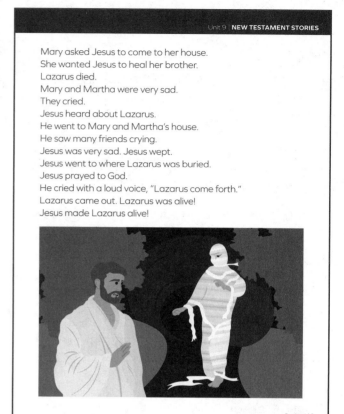

Unit 9 | **NEW TESTAMENT STORIES**

Mary asked Jesus to come to her house.
She wanted Jesus to heal her brother.
Lazarus died.
Mary and Martha were very sad.
They cried.
Jesus heard about Lazarus.
He went to Mary and Martha's house.
He saw many friends crying.
Jesus was very sad. Jesus wept.
Jesus went to where Lazarus was buried.
Jesus prayed to God.
He cried with a loud voice, "Lazarus come forth."
Lazarus came out. Lazarus was alive!
Jesus made Lazarus alive!

Section 1 | **3**

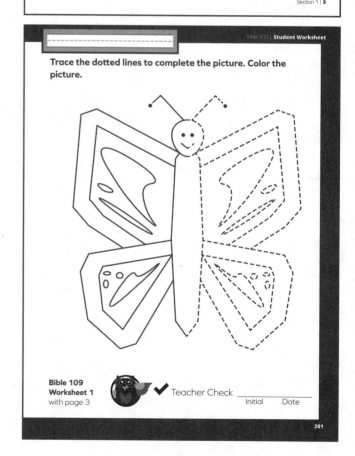

Bible 109 | **Student Worksheet**

Trace the dotted lines to complete the picture. Color the picture.

**Bible 109
Worksheet 1**
with page 3

✔ Teacher Check _____
Initial   Date

201

PAGES 4 AND 5: LAZARUS

MATERIALS NEEDED

- pencils
- Worksheet 2

Concepts:

Lazarus was a good friend of Jesus. Lazarus became very sick and died. Jesus raised Lazarus from the dead.

Teacher Goals:

To teach the children to review the story of Lazarus and to have them complete activities about the story.

Bible Reference:

John 11:1–44

Reading Integration:

Following directions, answering yes/no questions, past tense verbs (words that end in *ed*), antonyms (opposites), putting words in order to make complete sentences

Teaching Pages 4 and 5:

1. Review the story of Lazarus with the students. Read the directions on page 4 with the students. Assign page 4.

   Write the words *play* and *played* on the board. Ask the students to use each word in a sentence. Tell them that when the letters *ed* are added to an action word, it refers to something that was done in the past. Assign the top of page 5.

   Write on the board:
   > *tall — short*
   > *light — dark*
   > *day — night*

   Ask the students if they can find the relationship between these words. Explain that these words are opposites or antonyms. Assign the rest of page 5.

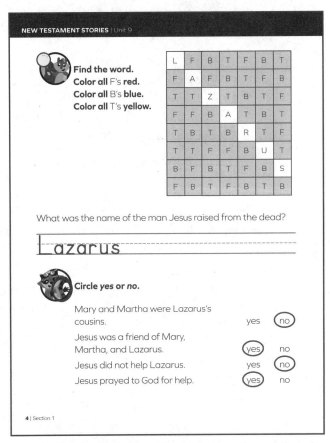

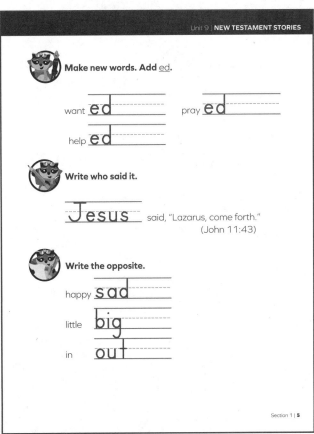

Activities:

1. Write these words on the board:

   Jesus Lazarus and friends were

   Ask the students if these words make a complete sentence. Do they make sense when they are written in this order? Ask the students to put these words in order to make a complete sentence.

   Write the sentence on the board:

   Jesus and Lazarus were friends.
   or
   Lazarus and Jesus were friends.

2. Read the directions for Worksheet 2 with the students. Tell the students that the answer for the first problem on the worksheet is on the board. Assign Worksheet 2.

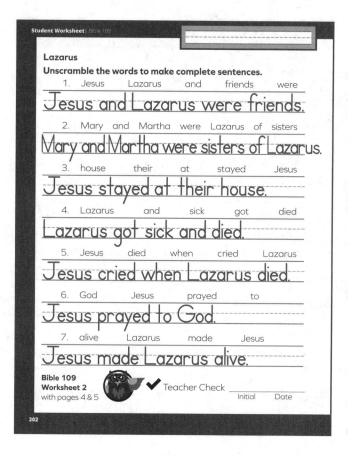

PAGE 6: THOMAS

MATERIALS NEEDED

- pencils
- Worksheet 3

Concepts:

Thomas was a disciple of Jesus. Being a disciple means "to follow."

Objectives:

Students will know some stories from the New Testament.

Students will know some men of the New Testament.

Teacher Goals:

To teach the children to begin to understand the meaning of *disciple* and the story of Thomas, to have them read about Thomas, and to have them participate in a game of "Follow the Leader" to help them comprehend the concept of a disciple.

Bible Reference:

John 20:24–31

Reading Integration:

Categorizing

Vocabulary:

Thomas, miracles, followed, disciple, touch

Teaching Page 6:

1. Begin the lesson with a simple game of "Follow the Leader" (with you, the teacher, as the leader). After playing this game with the students for several minutes, tell them to sit down. Tell them they are going to learn a new word. Write the word *disciple* on the board. Explain that a disciple is a follower. Write = *follower* next to the word *disciple*.

2. Explain to the students that Jesus had men who were his disciples. They heard Jesus talk and saw Jesus do miracles. They could ask Jesus questions. Explain to the students that they can be disciples of Jesus also by learning about Him, reading Bible stories, memorizing Bible verses, and praying to Him. Tell the students that they are going to read about Thomas, a disciple of Jesus.

NEW TESTAMENT STORIES | Unit 9

Thomas
(John 20:24–31)

Thomas was a friend of Jesus.
Thomas saw Lazarus.
Thomas saw Jesus do miracles.
Thomas listened to Jesus.
He followed Jesus.
He was a disciple of Jesus.
Thomas was sad when Jesus died on the cross.
He thought Jesus was gone.
The disciples told Thomas that they saw Jesus.
Thomas did not believe the disciples.
He said he needed to see Jesus.
He said he needed to touch Jesus.

| Thomas

6 | Section 1

Activities:

Look at the pictures on Worksheet 3 together. Read the four categories. Explain how the things are alike and can be placed in groups (or categories). Assign Worksheet 3.

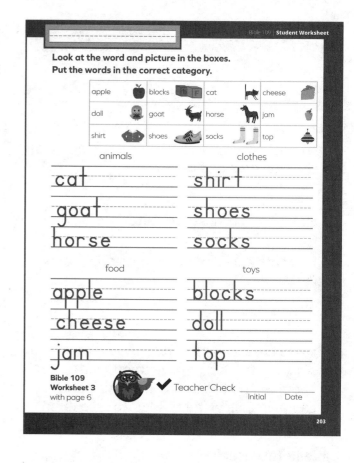

PAGE 7: THOMAS

MATERIALS NEEDED

- pencils
- Worksheet 4

Concepts:

Thomas did not believe that Jesus had risen from the dead. Thomas knew that Jesus was alive when he saw and talked to Jesus.

Objectives:

Students will know some stories from the New Testament.

Students will know some men of the New Testament.

Teacher Goal:

To teach the children to help them better understand the meaning of *disciple* and discuss the concept of doubt and to help them learn that Thomas doubted that Jesus was alive until he saw Him and touched Him.

Bible Reference:

John 20:24–31

Reading Integration:

Letter shapes in words

Vocabulary:

surprised, scars, alive

Teaching Page 7:

1. Ask the students what they remember about Thomas. Tell them that they are going to read more about Thomas.

2. Read page 7 with the students and discuss the illustration. Discuss the phrase "Doubting Thomas" with the students.

Activity:

Review the story of Thomas. Discuss the different shapes of letters with the students. Assign Worksheet 4.

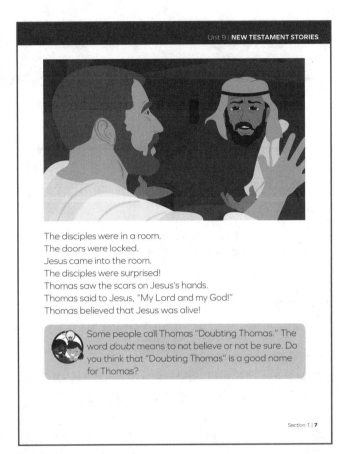

Unit 9 | NEW TESTAMENT STORIES

The disciples were in a room.
The doors were locked.
Jesus came into the room.
The disciples were surprised!
Thomas saw the scars on Jesus's hands.
Thomas said to Jesus, "My Lord and my God!"
Thomas believed that Jesus was alive!

Some people call Thomas "Doubting Thomas." The word *doubt* means to not believe or not be sure. Do you think that "Doubting Thomas" is a good name for Thomas?

Section 1 | **7**

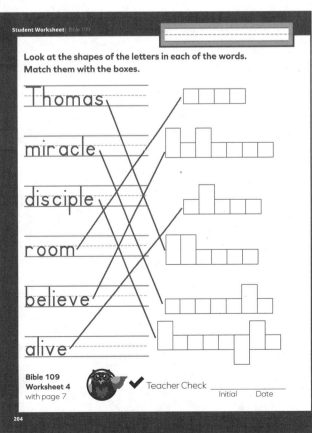

Student Worksheet | Bible 109

Look at the shapes of the letters in each of the words. Match them with the boxes.

Thomas
miracle
disciple
room
believe
alive

Bible 109
Worksheet 4
with page 7

Teacher Check _____
Initial   Date

204

171

PAGE 8: THOMAS—REVIEW

MATERIALS NEEDED

• pencils

Concepts:

Thomas was a disciple of Jesus. Being a follower is being a disciple. Thomas knew that Jesus was alive when he saw Jesus and talked to him.

Teacher Goals:

To teach the children to be able to orally tell the story of Thomas and to complete some fill-in-the-blank problems about Thomas.

Reading Integration:

Categorizing, short vowel sounds

Teaching Page 8:

Ask the students to tell you the story about Thomas. Ask them what the word *disciple* means. Assign page 8.

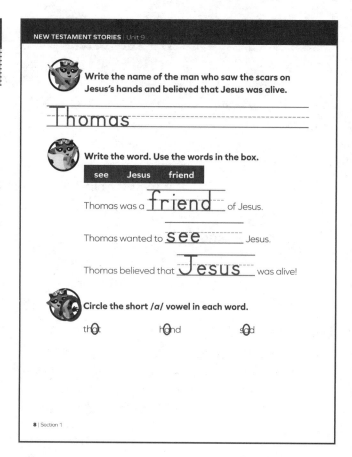

PAGE 9: STEPHEN

Concepts:

Stephen was a friend of God. Stephen believed that Jesus was God's son who died and rose from the dead.

Objectives:

Students will know some stories from the New Testament.

Students will know some men of the New Testament.

Teacher Goal:

To teach the children so they will be able to describe Stephen as someone who loved God.

Bible Refeerences:

Acts 6:8-15; 7:54-60

Vocabulary:

Stephen, angel, miracles, threw, afraid

Teaching Page 9:

Review with the students that Jesus did a miracle for Lazarus and that Thomas was a disciple of Jesus. Tell them that they are going to read about another follower of Jesus, Stephen. Read page 9 with the students.

Unit 9 | **NEW TESTAMENT STORIES**

Stephen
(Acts 6:8–15; 7:54–60)

| Stephen

Stephen loved God.
He believed that Jesus died for him.
He was God's friend.
Stephen told the people about Jesus.
Some people thought that Stephen looked like an angel.
God helped him do miracles.
Some men did not like Stephen.
They did not like what he said about God.
They decided to hurt Stephen.
The men threw stones at Stephen.
Stephen was not afraid.
He knew that God was with him.

Section 1 | **9**

PAGE 10: STEPHEN

MATERIALS NEEDED

- pencils
- Worksheet 5

Concepts:

Stephen was killed because he loved God and Jesus. Stephen knew he was going to heaven. Stephen was a martyr for Jesus.

Objectives:

Students will know some stories from the New Testament.

Students will know some men of the New Testament.

Teacher Goal:

To teach the children so they will be able to define the word *martyr* and tell that Stephen went to heaven.

Reading Integration:

Following/reading directions, letter shapes

Bible References:

Acts 6:8–15; 7:54–60

Vocabulary:

receive, heaven, martyr

Teaching Page 10:

1. Review with the students what they know about Stephen so far. Explain to them that Stephen was a disciple of Jesus. He was kind and obeyed Jesus.

2. Read page 10 together. Discuss with the students that Stephen loved Jesus and that when Stephen died he knew that he would be with Jesus in heaven (offer them this comfort from this story!). Read page 10 again, discussing the meaning of the word *martyr*.

Activity:

Explain to the students that it is very important to read and follow directions. Read the directions of Worksheet 5 with them. Assign Worksheet 5.

Stephen saw God in heaven.
He prayed, "Lord Jesus, receive my spirit."
Stephen died.
Stephen went to heaven.
Stephen died because he loved Jesus.
Stephen went to heaven because he loved Jesus.
A person who dies for his or her beliefs
is called a **martyr** (mar tur).
Stephen was the first Christian martyr.

10 | Section 1

Bible 109 | **Student Worksheet**

Find the Mystery Word. Use the words in the box to help you find the words that go in the boxes.

rose	mom	ant	toy	yellow	rug

1. another word for *mother* — mom
2. a small insect that lives in tunnels in the ground — ant
3. something that covers the floor — rug
4. something to play with like a doll or a truck — toy
5. the color of lemons and butter — yellow
6. a beautiful flower — rose

Now circle the first letter of the words you wrote in the boxes. Write the letters on the line. It will be the word that tells about Stephen.

martyr

**Bible 109
Worksheet 5**
with page 10

Teacher Check _____ _____
Initial   Date

205

PAGE 11: STEPHEN—REVIEW

MATERIALS NEEDED

- crayons
- pencils
- New Testament booklet
- Worksheet 6

Concepts:

Stephen was a friend of God and believed that Jesus was God's son who died and rose from the dead. Stephen was killed because he loved God. Stephen knew he was going to heaven. Stephen was a martyr for Jesus.

Teacher Goals:

To teach the children so they begin to memorize the Bible verse, Matthew 5:8 and after orally reviewing the story of Stephen, to be able to answer two problems about Thomas and Stephen.

Reading Integration:

Short vowel sounds

Bible References:

John 20:28; Acts 7:59

Teaching Page 11:

Review the stories about Thomas and Stephen with the students. Read the directions on page 11 with the students. Assign page 11.

Activity:

Tell the students to write the memory verse (Matthew 5:8) on Worksheet 6. Write the following in the New Testament booklet on page 2:

I read about these men of the New Testament:
   Lazarus
   Thomas
   Stephen

Suggested Song:

"In My Life, Be Glorified" (Words and music by Bob Kilpatrick, © Copyright 1978 Bob Kilpatrick Music)

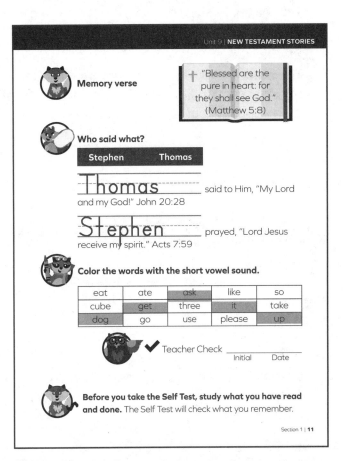

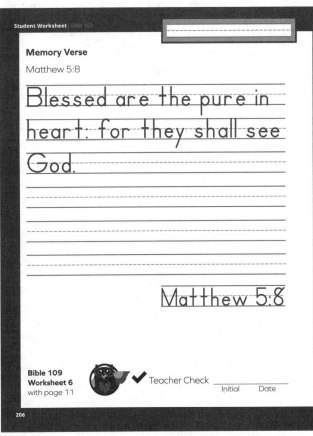

The students should prepare for the Self Test. Ask the students to look over and read the Self Test but they should not write the answers to any questions. After looking over the Self Test the students should go to the beginning of the unit and reread the text and review the answers to the activities up to the Self Test.

The students are to complete the Self Test the next school day. This should be done under regular test conditions without allowing the students to look back. A good idea is to clip the pages together before the test.

PAGE 12: SELF TEST 1

MATERIALS NEEDED

• pencils

Concept:

Evaluation.

Teacher Goal:

Evaluate student's knowledge of Lazarus, Thomas, Stephen, and the memory verse, Matthew 5:8.

Teaching Page 12:

Assign Self Test 1 and listen to recitation of Matthew 5:8.

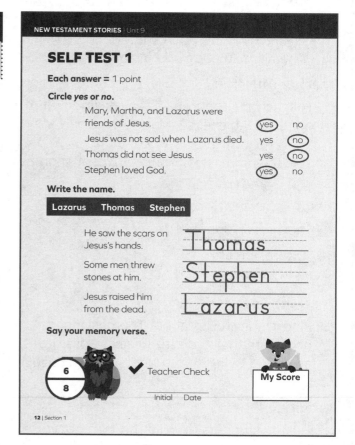

2. WOMEN OF THE NEW TESTAMENT

PAGE 13: MARY

Concepts:

Mary, Anna, and Lydia are women from the New Testament. Mary found out that she would have a baby and must give him the name of Jesus.

Objectives:

Students will know some stories from the New Testament.

Students will know some women of the New Testament.

Teacher Goal:

Introduce Mary, Anna, and Lydia as women from the New Testament.

Bible References:

Matthew 1:16–25; Luke 1:26–56, 2:1–24

Vocabulary:

Mary, Anna, Lydia, angel, young, Gabriel, scared, Savior

Unit 9 | **NEW TESTAMENT STORIES**

2. WOMEN OF THE NEW TESTAMENT

You will read about Mary, Jesus's mother.
You will read about Anna.
You will read about Lydia.
You will learn how God helped these women.

Mary

(Matthew 1:16–25; Luke 1:26–56 & 2:1–24)

God sent an angel to talk to a young girl.
Gabriel was the angel.
Mary was the young girl.
Mary was scared when she saw Gabriel.
Gabriel told her not to be scared.
He told Mary that she was very special.
She was going to have a baby boy.
Her baby boy would be the Savior.
The baby was to be named Jesus.
He would save God's children.

| Mary

Section 2 | **13**

Teaching Page 13:

1. Ask the students who the three men of the New Testament that they recently read about are. (Lazarus, Thomas, and Stephen) Write these names on the board: *Mary, Anna, Lydia.* Tell the students that these are women of the New Testament that they will be reading about.

2. Read the top of page 13 together. Tell the students that they are going to read about Mary.

3. Write the word *angel* on the board. Tell them that an angel is a messenger from God. Tell them that they are going to read about the angel Gabriel. Tell them that they will read about who Gabriel talked to. Read the rest of page 13 together.

PAGE 14: MARY

MATERIALS NEEDED

- pencils
- Worksheet 7

Concepts:

Mary had a baby boy and named him Jesus. Angels told some shepherds about Jesus and they came to see him. Jesus's birthday was the first Christmas.

Objectives:

Students will know some stories from the New Testament.

Students will know some women of the New Testament.

Teacher Goal:

To teach the children to tell the story of the first Christmas.

Bible References:

Matthew 1:16–25; Luke 1:26–56, 2:1–24

Vocabulary:

Joseph, Bethlehem, stable, animals, manger, straw, worship, Christmas

Teaching Page 14:

Review what was read so far about Mary. Read page 14 together. Discuss the first Christmas.

Activity:

Read the directions of Worksheet 7 with the students. Assign Worksheet 7.

NEW TESTAMENT STORIES | Unit 9

Mary praised God for the good news of Jesus.
She married Joseph.
They went to Bethlehem.
They could not find a place to stay.
They had to stay in a stable.
A stable is where animals were fed.
Baby Jesus was born in the stable.
Mary laid him in a manger.
The straw kept baby Jesus warm.
Angels told some shepherds about Jesus.
The shepherds came to the stable to worship Jesus.
Everyone was glad that Jesus was born!
This was the very first Christmas.

14 | Section 2

Bible 109 | **Student Worksheet**

a	b	c	d	e	f	g	h	i	j	k	l	m	n	o	p	q	r	s	t	u	v	w	x	y	z
1	2	3	4	5	6	7	8	9	10	11	12	13	14	15	16	17	18	19	20	21	22	23	24	25	26

Use the numbers and letters above to solve the riddle.

1. What is the day that we celebrate the birthday of Jesus?

c	h	r	i	s	t	m	a	s
3	8	18	9	19	20	13	1	19

2. Now use the numbers and letters to write the numbers for the word.

b	i	r	t	h	d	a	y
2	9	18	20	8	4	1	25

When is your birthday? Write the date of your birthday on the line.

------------------Teacher check------------------

**Bible 109
Worksheet 7**
with page 14

✔ Teacher Check _____ _____
Initial   Date

207

PAGE 15: MARY—REVIEW

Concepts:

Mary had a baby boy and named him Jesus. Angels told some shepherds about Jesus and they came to see him. Jesus's birthday was the first Christmas.

Teacher Goals:

To teach the children so they can complete some problems about Mary and to learn the meaning of the word *Savior*.

Bible References:

Matthew 1:16–25; Luke 1:26–56, 2:1–24

Teaching Page 15:

1. Ask the students to tell you the story of Mary. Go over the directions on page 15. Assign page 15.

2. Read the discussion question on the bottom of page 15 together. Write the word *Savior* on the board. Say the word *Savior* slowly. Ask the students what they think the main word of *Savior* would be.

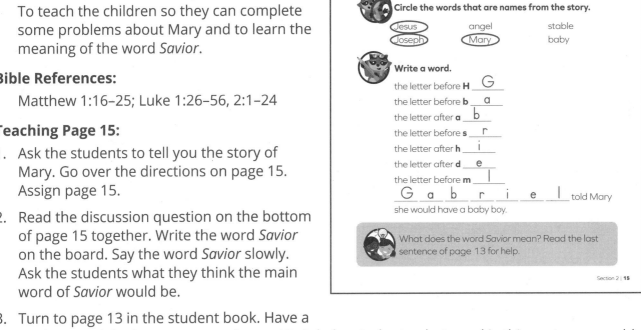

3. Turn to page 13 in the student book. Have a student read the last sentence of page 13. Ask the students what word in this sentence would go with the word *Savior*. Explain to the students that the word *Savior* means "someone who saves." Jesus is our Savior. He saves us from our sins.

PAGE 16: ACTIVITY—THE FIRST CHRISTMAS

Concept:

The first Christmas.

Teacher Goal:

To teach the children to draw a picture about the first Christmas.

Teaching Page 16:

Discuss with the students some of the things that were present at the first Christmas. Tell them to draw a picture of the first Christmas on page 16.

Suggested Song:

"Away in a Manger"

PAGES 17 AND 18: ANNA

Concepts:

Anna was a prophetess who was waiting in the temple to see baby Jesus. She was very happy when she finally got to see baby Jesus.

Objectives:

Students will know some stories from the New Testament.

Students will know some women of the New Testament.

Teacher Goal:

Read the story of Anna with the children and help them remember the story.

Bible Reference:

Luke 2:21–38

Vocabulary:

prophetess, husband, temple, dedicate

Teaching Pages 17 and 18:

1. Ask the students if they remember what a prophet is. Write the word *prophet* on the board. Now write the word *prophetess* next to the word prophet. Ask how the two words are alike. Explain to the students that a prophetess is a woman prophet. They are going to read about a prophetess. This prophetess is Anna.

2. Read pages 17 and 18 together. Discuss the illustration on page 18.

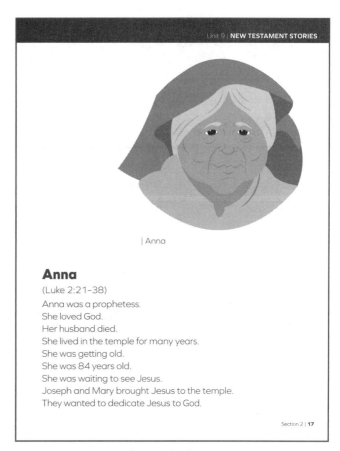

Unit 9 | NEW TESTAMENT STORIES

| Anna

Anna

(Luke 2:21–38)

Anna was a prophetess.
She loved God.
Her husband died.
She lived in the temple for many years.
She was getting old.
She was 84 years old.
She was waiting to see Jesus.
Joseph and Mary brought Jesus to the temple.
They wanted to dedicate Jesus to God.

Section 2 | 17

NEW TESTAMENT STORIES | Unit 9

Anna was in the temple.
She held Jesus.
She was so happy to see Jesus.
She gave thanks to God.
She told many people about Jesus.

18 | Section 2

PAGES 19 AND 20: ANNA—REVIEW

MATERIALS NEEDED

- pencils
- Worksheets 8 and 9

Concepts:

Anna was a prophetess who was waiting in the temple to see baby Jesus. She was very happy when she finally got to see baby Jesus.

Teacher Goals:

Introduce the memory verse, Matthew 1:21, and assist the children in completing a review page about Anna.

Reading Integration:

Distinguishing words that mean the same (synonyms) and words that mean the opposite (antonyms)

Bible Reference:

Luke 2:21–38

Teaching Pages 19 and 20:

1. Review with the students what they have read so far about Anna and Mary. Read the memory verse together. Assign page 19.

2. Assign page 20. Write the word *happy* on the board. Tell students to think about words that mean the same as the word happy. Then have the students think about some words that mean the opposite of happy. Allow students time to complete the second activity on page 20 and then make the following statement.

   Say:

   "Read the words that are not colored."
   "What is alike about these words?"
   (All of the words rhyme, or all of the words end in *all*.)

3. Go over the instructions for the yes/no questions about Anna and Mary and allow students time to complete the activity.

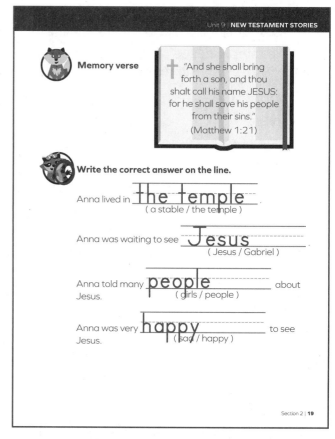

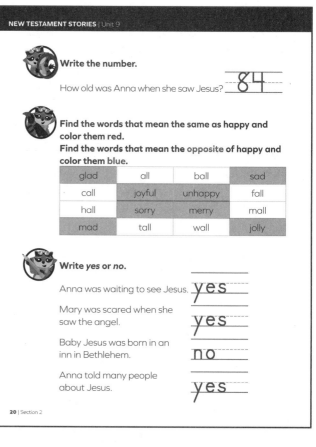

Activities:

1. Tell students to write the memory verse (Matthew 1:21) on Worksheet 8.

2. Read the directions of Worksheet 9 together.

   Say:

   "These words are spelled the same forwards as well as backwards! These kinds of words are called *palindromes*." (Write the word *palindrome* on the board.) "Isn't *palindrome* a big word? But palindrome words are easy to spell! You can spell a palindrome backwards and it is still correct!"

3. Demonstrate some examples on the board: *deed, did, dud, eve, eye, mum, peep, pup, sis, tot, toot, wow.*

4. Assign Worksheet 9.

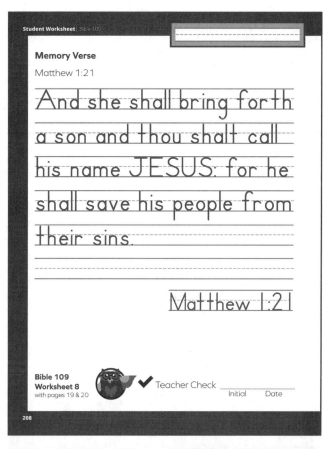

PAGES 21 AND 22: LYDIA

MATERIALS NEEDED

- pencils
- purple crayon
- New Testament booklet
- Worksheet 10

Concepts:

Lydia was a business woman who made and sold purple cloth. She believed in Jesus and helped Paul.

Objectives:

Students will know some stories from the New Testament.

Students will know some women of the New Testament.

Teacher Goal:

Assist the children in being able to tell the story of Lydia of the New Testament.

Reading Integration:

Following directions

Bible References:

Acts 16:14–15; 40

Vocabulary:

business, costly, Christian, baptized, prison

Teaching Pages 21 and 22:

1. Tell the students that they will be reading about Lydia from the New Testament. She was an important business woman.

2. Read page 21 together. *Say:* "Did you know that to make the purple dye for the cloth, Lydia had to crush the shells of many tiny sea creatures? The cloth was costly because it was difficult to make the dye to color the cloth purple."

3. Discuss different types of clothing with the students. Assign page 22.

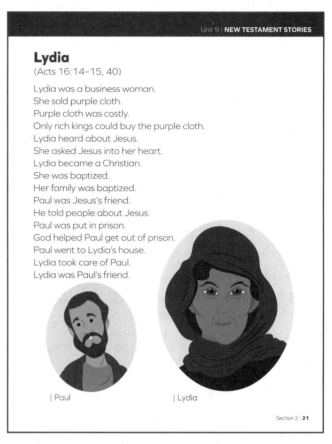

Activity:

1. Read the directions on Worksheet 10 with the students. Assign Worksheet 10.

2. Write the following in the New Testament booklet (page 3):

   I read about these women of the New Testament:

   > *Mary*
   > *Anna*
   > *Lydia*

The students should prepare for the Self Test. Ask the students to look over and read the Self Test but they should not write the answers to any questions. After looking over the Self Test the students should go to the beginning of the unit and reread the text and review the answers to the activities up to the Self Test.

The students are to complete the Self Test the next school day. This should be done under regular test conditions without allowing the students to look back. A good idea is to clip the pages together before the test.

PAGE 23: SELF TEST 2

MATERIALS NEEDED

• pencils

Concept:

Evaluation.

Teacher Goal:

Evaluate students' knowledge of Mary, Anna, Lydia, and the memory verse, Matthew 1:21.

Teaching Page 23:

Assign Self Test 2 and listen to recitation of Matthew 1:21.

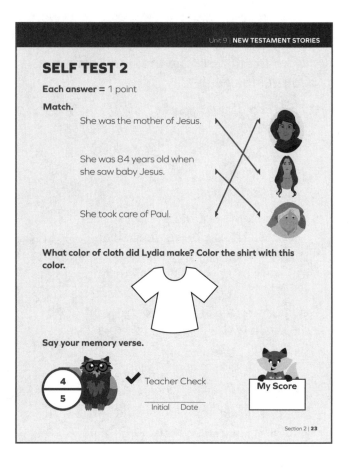

3. CHILDREN OF THE NEW TESTAMENT

PAGE 24: AN OFFICIAL'S SON

MATERIALS NEEDED

- pencils
- Worksheet 11

Concept:

An official's son, Jesus and the children, and Eutychus are children from the New Testament.

Objectives:

Students will know some stories from the New Testament.

Students will know some children of the New Testament.

Teacher Goals:

To teach the children to learn about an official's son, Jesus and the children, and Eutychus who were children in the New Testament and to read about an official's son who was very sick.

Bible Reference:

John 4:43–54

Reading Integration:

Word families

Vocabulary:

official, important, believe

NEW TESTAMENT STORIES | Unit 9

3. CHILDREN OF THE NEW TESTAMENT

You will read about an official's son.
You will read about Jesus and some children.
You will read about a boy
who fell asleep during church.
You will learn that God loves children.

An Official's Son
(John 4:43–54)

An important man came to Jesus.
His son was very sick.
He thought his son would die.
The man begged Jesus to heal his son.
Jesus told him that his son was healed.
The man believed Jesus and went home.

| Official

24 | Section 3

Teaching Page 24:

1. Review the men and women of the New Testament (Lazarus, Thomas, Stephen, Mary, Anna, and Lydia) with the students. Tell the students that they will be learning about some children from the New Testament. Read the top of page 24 together.

2. Tell the students that they will be reading about the son of an official. An official is a very important man. Read the bottom of page 24 together.

Activity:

Write the words *boat*, *coat*, and *goat* on the board. Ask the students how these words are alike. Explain to them that these words are from the word family *oat*. These words all rhyme with *oat*. Read the directions of Worksheet 11. Assign Worksheet 11.

PAGE 25: AN OFFICIAL'S SON

Concepts:

An official's son was very sick. He went to Jesus for help. Jesus healed the son. The official and his family believed that Jesus was God's son.

Objectives:

Students will know some stories from the New Testament.

Students will know some children of the New Testament.

Teacher Goals:

To teach the children to be able to read how an official's son was healed by Jesus and to read how the official and his family believed that Jesus was God's Son.

Bible Reference:

John 4:43–54

Vocabulary:

alive, household

Teaching Page 25:

1. Tell the students that they will be reading about how Jesus healed the official's son. An official is a very important man.

2. Discuss the illustration on page 25, and then read page 25 together.

Unit 9 | **NEW TESTAMENT STORIES**

The man's servants met the man on the road.
They told him that his son was alive.
The man asked what time his son was healed.
They told him it was at one o'clock.
The man knew that was the time Jesus
told him that his son was healed.
So the man and his household believed in Jesus.

Section 3 | **25**

PAGE 26: AN OFFICIAL'S SON—REVIEW

MATERIALS NEEDED

- pencils
- Worksheet 12

Concepts:

An official's son was very sick. He went to Jesus for help. Jesus healed the son. The official and his family believed that Jesus was God's son.

Teacher Goal:

To teach the children to be able to complete review activities about the story of the official's son after oral review of the story.

Bible Reference:

John 4:43–54

Teaching Page 26:

1. Review with the students the story of the official's son. Introduce and discuss the memory verse on page 26. Explain any unfamiliar word usages to the students; e.g., *suffer* in this usage means "to let or allow."

2. Have the students read the discussion question. Ask them what they would have done if they were the official.

3. Assign the three problems at the bottom of page 26.

Activity:

Tell students to write the memory verse, Mark 10:14b, on Worksheet 12.

Suggested Song:

"My God is So Great, So Strong, and So Mighty"

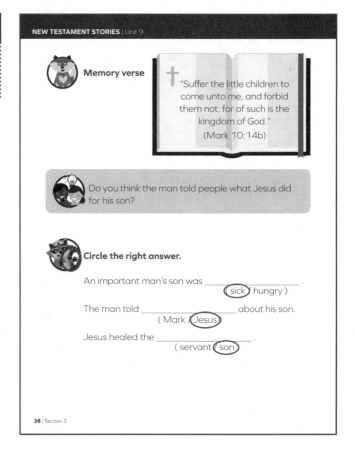

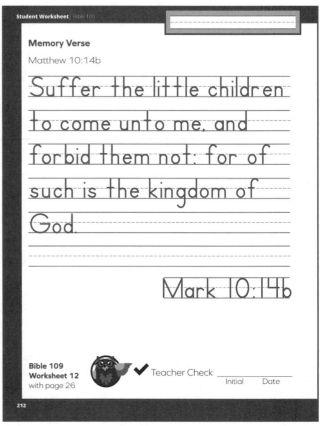

PAGE 27: JESUS AND THE LITTLE CHILDREN

MATERIALS NEEDED

- pencils
- Worksheet 13

Concept:

Jesus told the disciples to let the children come to Him.

Objectives:

Students will know some stories from the New Testament.

Students will know some children of the New Testament.

Teacher Goal:

To teach the children to be able to read and understand that Jesus wanted to talk to the children.

Bible Reference:

Mark 10:13–16

Teaching Page 27:

Tell the students that they are going to read how Jesus loved the children. Read page 27 together. Ask them to repeat the words that Jesus said. Tell them that these words are their memory verse. Discuss the meanings of *suffer* and *forbid*.

Activity:

Assign the maze on Worksheet 13.

Unit 9 | **NEW TESTAMENT STORIES**

Jesus and the Little Children
(Mark 10:13–16)

Jesus went to many towns to tell
the people about God.
Many people went to listen to Jesus.
Some people took their children to Jesus.
The people wanted Jesus to touch the children.
They knew that Jesus was powerful.
Jesus's friends did not want the children
to be close to Jesus.
They told them to go away.
But Jesus wanted to be with the children.
He said, "Suffer the little children to come
unto me, and forbid them not:
for of such is the kingdom of God."
Then Jesus took the children in His arms.
He put his hands on them.
He blessed them.

Section 3 | **27**

Bible 109 | **Student Worksheet**

Help take the children to Jesus.

Bible 109
Worksheet 13
with page 27

Teacher Check _____
Initial   Date

213

PAGE 28: JESUS AND THE LITTLE CHILDREN—REVIEW

Concept:

Jesus told the disciples to let the children come to Him.

Objectives:

Students will know some stories from the New Testament.

Students will know some children of the New Testament.

Teacher Goal:

To teach the children to be able to, after oral review of the story of the official's son, answer four problems about Jesus and the little children.

Bible Reference:

Mark 10:13–16

Teaching Page 28:

Review with the students the story of Jesus and the little children. Assign page 28.

Suggested Songs:

"Children, Children" (Words & music by Robert C. Evans, © Copyright 1982 Integrity's Hosanna! Music)

"Jesus Loves the Little Children" (By Rev. C.H. Woolston and George F. Root)

PAGE 29: THE BOY WHO FELL ASLEEP IN CHURCH (EUTYCHUS)

Concepts:

Paul loved Jesus and told many people about Him. One night he talked about Jesus for a very long time—past midnight!

Objectives:

Students will know some stories from the New Testament.

Students will know some children of the New Testament.

Teacher Goal:

Read with the children about Paul and Eutychus.

Bible Reference:

Acts 20:7–12

Vocabulary:

Paul, upstairs, midnight, Eutychus, window

Teaching Page 29:

Tell the students that Paul loved Jesus. He liked to tell other people about Jesus. Read page 29 together. Discuss the illustration on page 29.

Unit 9 | **NEW TESTAMENT STORIES**

The Boy Who Fell Asleep in Church
(Acts 20:7–12)

Paul loved Jesus.
He liked to tell people about Jesus.
One day, Paul was talking to some people in an upstairs room.
He spoke a very long time.
Soon it was midnight.
Eutychus (yoo ti kus) was a young man listening to Paul.
He was sitting on a window sill.

Section 3 | **29**

PAGE 30: THE BOY WHO FELL ASLEEP IN CHURCH (EUTYCHUS)

MATERIALS NEEDED

- pencils
- Worksheet 14

Concepts:

Eutychus was listening to Paul. He fell asleep and fell out of the window. God gave Paul the power to heal Eutychus.

Objectives:

Students will know some stories from the New Testament.

Students will know some children of the New Testament.

Teacher Goals:

Read with the children about how Eutychus fell out of the window and died and how God helped Paul make Eutychus alive again.

Bible Reference:

Acts 20:7–12

Vocabulary:

ground, worry

Teaching Page 30:

Review with the students who Paul is. Write the name *Eutychus* on the board. Tell the students that something unusual happened to Eutychus. Read page 30 and discuss the illustration.

Activity:

Read the directions for Worksheet 14. Assign Worksheet 14.

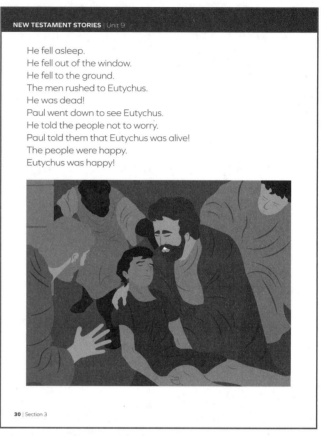

NEW TESTAMENT STORIES | Unit 9

He fell asleep.
He fell out of the window.
He fell to the ground.
The men rushed to Eutychus.
He was dead!
Paul went down to see Eutychus.
He told the people not to worry.
Paul told them that Eutychus was alive!
The people were happy.
Eutychus was happy!

30 | Section 3

Student Worksheet | Bible 109

Read the clues. Read the words in the box.
Write the words in the puzzle.

| alive | in | listening | sleep | window |

1. Eutychus was __listening__ to Paul.
2. Eutychus was tired and went to __sleep__.
3. Eutychus fell out of a __window__.
4. God made Eutychus __alive__ again.
5. The people believed __in__ God.

Bible 109
Worksheet 14
with page 30

Teacher Check _____
Initial   Date

214

PAGE 31: THE BOY WHO FELL ASLEEP IN CHURCH (EUTYCHUS)— REVIEW

MATERIALS NEEDED

- pencils
- New Testament booklet

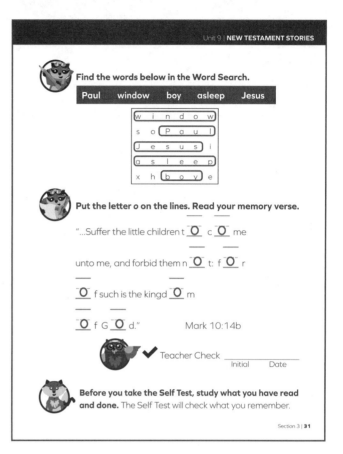

Concepts:

Paul loved Jesus and told many people about him. One night he talked about Jesus for a very long time—past midnight! Eutychus was listening to Paul. He fell asleep and fell out of the window. God gave Paul the power to heal Eutychus.

Teacher Goal:

To teach the children to be able to, after oral review of the story about Eutychus, complete a word search for this story.

Bible Reference:

Acts 20:7–12

Teaching Page 31:

Orally review the story of Eutychus and review the memory verse, Mark 10:14b. Assign page 31.

Activities:

Write in the "New Testament" booklet on page 4 the following:

I read about these children of the New Testament:

> *An official's son*
> *Jesus and the little children*
> *Eutychus*

The students should prepare for the Self Test. Ask the students to look over and read the Self Test but they should not write the answers to any questions. After looking over the Self Test the students should go to the beginning of the unit and reread the text and review the answers to the activities up to the Self Test.

The students are to complete the Self Test the next school day. This should be done under regular test conditions without allowing the students to look back. A good idea is to clip the pages together before the test.

PAGES 32 AND 33: SELF TEST 3

MATERIALS NEEDED

• pencils

Concept:

Evaluation.

Teacher Goal:

Evaluate student's knowledge of men of the New Testament, women of the New Testament, an official's son, Jesus and the children, Eutychus, and the memory verse, Mark 10:14b.

Teaching Pages 32 and 33:

Assign Self Test 3 and listen to recitation of Mark 10:14b and the other memory verses.

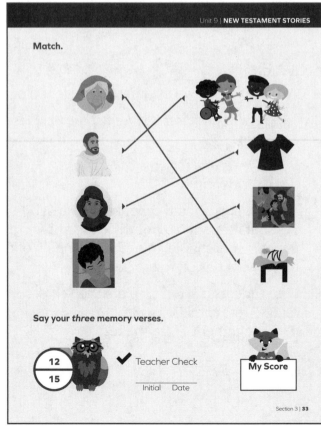

LIFEPAC TEST 109

Administer the test to the class as a group. Ask to have directions read or read them to the class. In either case, be sure that the children clearly understand. Put examples on the board if it seems necessary. Give ample time for each activity to be completed before going to the next.

Correct immediately and discuss with the child.

Review any concepts that have been missed.

Give those children who do not achieve the 80% score additional copies of the worksheets and a list of vocabulary words to study. A parent or a classroom helper should help in the review.

When the child is ready, give the Alternate LIFEPAC Test. Use the same procedure as for the LIFEPAC Test.

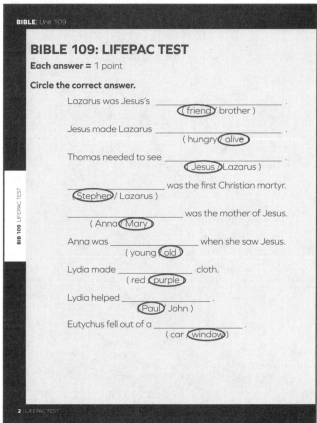

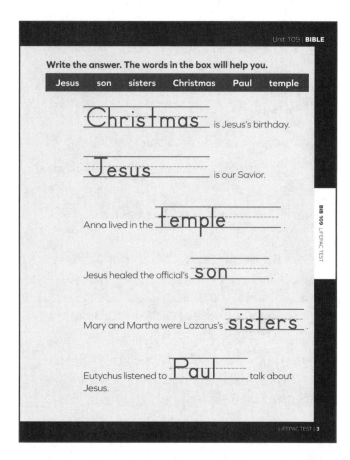

Write the answer. The words in the box will help you.

| Jesus | son | sisters | Christmas | Paul | temple |

__Christmas__ is Jesus's birthday.

__Jesus__ is our Savior.

Anna lived in the __temple__ .

Jesus healed the official's __son__ .

Mary and Martha were Lazarus's __sisters__ .

Eutychus listened to __Paul__ talk about Jesus.

BIB 109 LIFEPAC TEST

LIFEPAC TEST | **3**

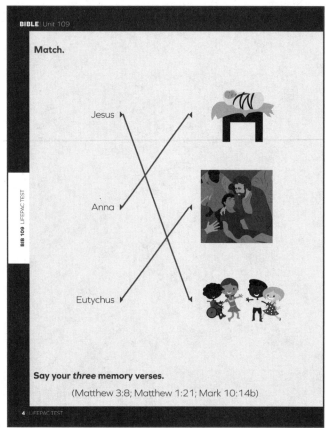

Match.

Jesus

Anna

Eutychus

BIB 109 LIFEPAC TEST

Say your *three* memory verses.

(Matthew 3:8; Matthew 1:21; Mark 10:14b)

4 | LIFEPAC TEST

ALTERNATE LIFEPAC TEST 109

Administer the test to the class as a group. Ask to have directions read or read them to the class. In either case, be sure that the children clearly understand. Put examples on the board if it seems necessary. Give ample time for each activity to be completed before going to the next.

Correct immediately and discuss with the child.

Review any concepts that have been missed.

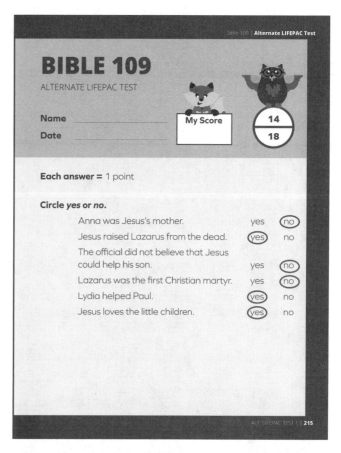

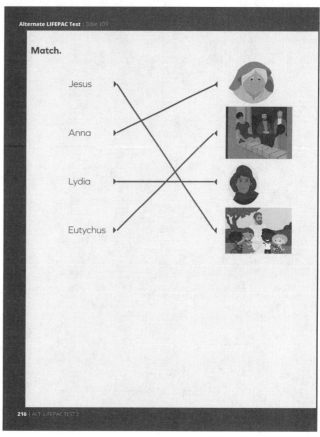

Trace the dotted lines to complete the picture. Color the picture.

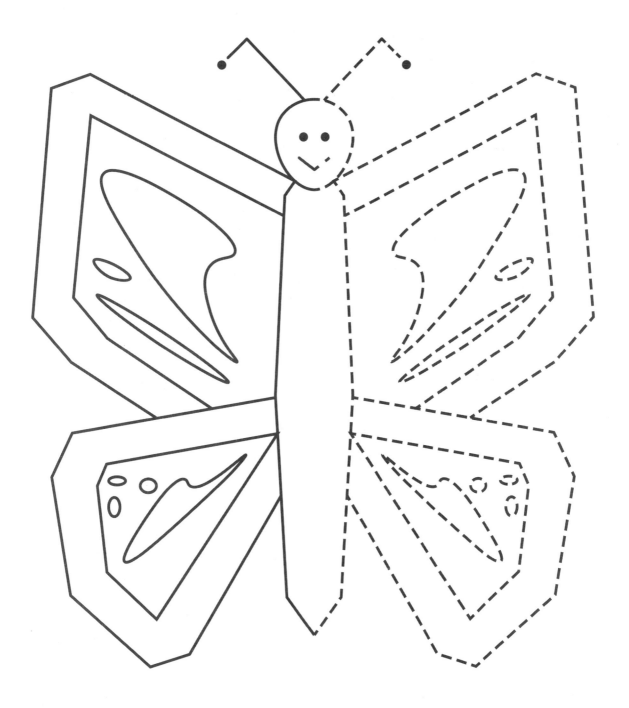

**Bible 109
Worksheet 1**
with page 3

Teacher Check _____
Initial   Date

Lazarus

Unscramble the words to make complete sentences.

1.   Jesus   Lazarus   and   friends   were

2.   Mary   and   Martha   were   Lazarus   of   sisters

3.   house   their   at   stayed   Jesus

4.   Lazarus   and   sick   got   died

5.   Jesus   died   when   cried   Lazarus

6.   God   Jesus   prayed   to

7.   alive   Lazarus   made   Jesus

Bible 109
Worksheet 2
with pages 4 & 5

✔ Teacher Check _____

Initial   Date

Look at the word and picture in the boxes.
Put the words in the correct category.

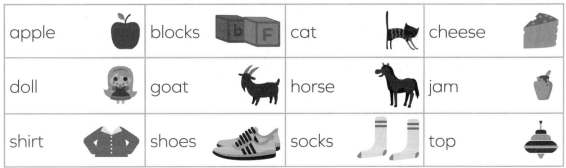

apple		blocks		cat		cheese	
doll		goat		horse		jam	
shirt		shoes		socks		top	

animals

clothes

food

toys

Teacher Check _____
Initial   Date

Look at the shapes of the letters in each of the words. Match them with the boxes.

Thomas

miracle

disciple

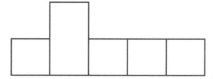

room

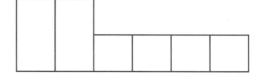

believe

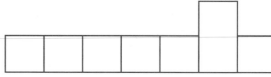

alive

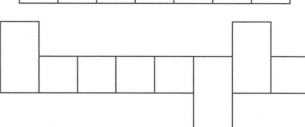

Bible 109
Worksheet 4
with page 7

Teacher Check _____

Initial   Date

Find the Mystery Word. Use the words in the box to help you find the words that go in the boxes.

rose	mom	ant	toy	yellow	rug

1. another word for *mother*

2. a small insect that lives in tunnels in the ground

3. something that covers the floor

4. something to play with like a doll or a truck

5. the color of lemons and butter

6. a beautiful flower

Now circle the first letter of the words you wrote in the boxes. Write the letters on the line. It will be the word that tells about Stephen.

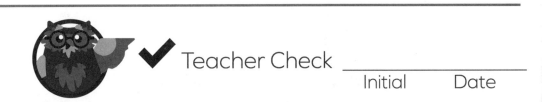

Bible 109
Worksheet 5
with page 10

✔ Teacher Check _____
                    Initial   Date

Memory Verse

Matthew 5:8

Bible 109
Worksheet 6
with page 11

✔ Teacher Check _____

Initial   Date

----

a	b	c	d	e	f	g	h	i	j	k	l	m	n	o	p	q	r	s	t	u	v	w	x	y	z
1	2	3	4	5	6	7	8	9	10	11	12	13	14	15	16	17	18	19	20	21	22	23	24	25	26

Use the numbers and letters above to solve the riddle.

1. What is the day that we celebrate the birthday of Jesus?

3	8	18	9	19	20	13	1	19

2. Now use the numbers and letters to write the numbers for the word.

b	i	r	t	h	d	a	y

When is your birthday? Write the date of your birthday on the line.

_____

_____

_____

**Bible 109
Worksheet 7**
with page 14

✔ Teacher Check _____
                              Initial   Date

Memory Verse

Matthew 1:21

Teacher Check _____

Initial   Date

Fun with Words!

Look at the name *Anna*. Did you notice that you can spell *Anna* backwards and it is still spelled correctly?

Let's have some fun with words! Read the words and then write them backwards on the line.

noon

_____

dad

_____

mom

_____

bib

_____

eye

_____

pop

_____

mum

_____

Bible 109
Worksheet 9
with pages 19 & 20

Color the letters with the △s purple to see who helped Paul by making cloth.

**Bible 109
Worksheet 10**
with page 21

Teacher Check _____

Initial   Date

210

Read the words. Look at the last three letters of each word. Put the words with the correct word family.

bite	pine	name	poke	white	joke
line	same	nine	game	woke	kite

ite

oke

ine

ame

✔ Teacher Check _____
Initial   Date

211

Memory Verse

Matthew 10:14b

Bible 109
Worksheet 12
with page 26

Teacher Check _____

Initial   Date

Help take the children to Jesus.

✔ Teacher Check _____

Initial   Date

Read the clues. Read the words in the box.
Write the words in the puzzle.

alive	in	listening	sleep	window

1. Eutychus was _____ to Paul.

2. Eutychus was tired and went to _____ .

3. Eutychus fell out of a _____ .

4. God made Eutychus _____ again.

5. The people believed _____ God.

Bible 109
Worksheet 14
with page 30

Teacher Check _____
Initial   Date

BIBLE 109

ALTERNATE LIFEPAC TEST

Name _____

Date _____

My Score

14 / 18

Each answer = 1 point

Circle *yes* or *no*.

Anna was Jesus's mother.	yes	no
Jesus raised Lazarus from the dead.	yes	no
The official did not believe that Jesus could help his son.	yes	no
Lazarus was the first Christian martyr.	yes	no
Lydia helped Paul.	yes	no
Jesus loves the little children.	yes	no

Match.

Jesus ▶   ◀

Anna ▶   ◀

Lydia ▶   ◀

Eutychus ▶   ◀

Write the answer. The words in the box will help you.

son	Thomas	Paul	Jesus	Lazarus

_____
_ _
_____ did not believe that

Jesus was alive.

                                                    _____
                                                    _ _ _ _ _ _ _ _ _
Jesus healed an important man's _____ .

                                  _____
                                  _ _ _ _ _ _ _ _ _ _ _ _ _ _ _ _ _ _ _
Anna wanted to see _____ .

                                            _____
                                            _ _ _ _ _ _ _ _ _ _ _ _ _ _
Eutychus fell asleep listening to _____ .

                        _____
                        _ _ _ _ _ _ _ _ _ _ _ _ _
Jesus raised _____ from the dead.

Say your three memory verses.

(Matthew 3:8; Matthew 1:21; Mark 10:14b)

BIBLE 110

Unit 10: God's World

GOD GAVE YOU MANY GIFTS
BIBLE 110

Alpha Omega
PUBLICATIONS

804 N. 2nd Ave. E.
Rock Rapids, IA 51246-1759

Author:
Mary Ellen Quint, Ph.D.
Pam Slagter, B.A.

Editor:
Alan Christopherson, M.S.

Media Credits:
Page 1: © stock_shoppe, iStock, Thinkstock;
6: © Kyrylo Polyanskyy, iStock, Thinkstock;
21: © stockakia, iStock, Thinkstock.

|i

PAGE 1: GOD GAVE YOU MANY GIFTS

MATERIALS NEEDED

- pencils
- writing tablet

Concept:

Review of Bible LIFEPACs.

Objective:

To introduce all the objectives.

Teacher Goal:

To review with the children Bible materials taught in Bible 101 through 109.

Reading Integration:

Main idea, listening

Vocabulary:

(Creation, Bible)
Note: Vocabulary words in parentheses were previously introduced and are being reviewed.

Teaching Page 1:

Have a child read the title. Ask the children to name all the things God has given them.

Have a volunteer read the first paragraph. Ask the children to recall what they can from the LIFEPACs.

Read the last two paragraphs to the children. Explain what a review is and what they will be doing in this LIFEPAC.

Have the children read the objectives silently. Have them read the objectives aloud. Discuss each objective and have the children recall briefly what they have learned about each.

Activity:

Have the children copy the objectives into their writing tablets.

Unit 10 | GOD GAVE YOU MANY GIFTS

GOD GAVE YOU MANY GIFTS

God gave you the whole world.
He gave you His Word, the Bible.
Best of all, God gave you His Son to save you.

You have learned about all of these gifts.
You have learned, too, how to thank God for them.

In this LIFEPAC®, you will review all of these things.

Objectives

Read these objectives. They will tell what you will be able to do when you have finished this LIFEPAC®.

1. I can tell about God's Creation.
2. I can tell how to show my love for God.
3. I can tell about God's Word.
4. I can tell what Jesus did.
5. I can tell how to pray.
6. I can tell about God's love.

Introduction | 1

1. GOD'S WORLD

PAGE 2: GOD CREATED ALL THINGS

MATERIALS NEEDED

• Bible

Concept:

God created all things.

Objective:

I can tell about God's creation.

Teacher Goal:

To review with the children God's creation of the World.

Bible References:

Genesis chapters 1 and 2

Reading Integration:

Main idea, listening, recalling details

Vocabulary:

(created, heaven, earth, land, sea, birds, plants, animals, Adam, Eve)
Note: Vocabulary words in parentheses were previously introduced and are being reviewed.

Teaching Page 2:

Read Genesis 1 and 2 as a review.

Ask a child to read the title and paragraph at the top of the page. Tell them that in this section, they will review Bible LIFEPACs 101, 102, 103, and 104. Have the children check the table of contents to see what they will learn in Section 1 and where they will find it.

Talk about the pictures on the page. Have the children identify the day of Creation on which each was made.

Have the children read the three paragraphs silently.

Read each paragraph aloud and discuss it in relation to the corresponding verses in Genesis 1 and 2.

PAGE 3: ACTIVITY PAGE

MATERIALS NEEDED	
• pencils	• Bible 101
• writing tablet	• Worksheet 1

Teaching Page 3:

One memory verse from each of the first nine LlFEPACs has been selected for this LIFEPAC. The memory verse on this page is from Bible 101. The children should recall this verse without much review work. Give help as required.

Discuss the memory verse by going back through Bible 101 with the children and recalling all they learned in that LIFEPAC.

Read the direction for the first activity. Let the children complete the activity independently. Check together and discuss the answers. If an answer is *no*, ask the children how they would have to change the statement to make it a *yes* statement.

Read the last direction. Ask the children to repeat it. Limit the list to one full page. Help with spelling as needed.

Activities:

1. Review booklets, Worksheets, and project activities for Bible 101.

2. Begin a class prayer book. Have the class compose a prayer thanking God for the things they have listed. Write the prayer on chart paper. Have the children make a border of things they listed. Use the chart as a wall hanging or bulletin display.

3. Do Worksheet 1.

    Read the directions. Make sure the children know what each picture is.

    Read Genesis 1 to the children and tell them to listen very carefully for the day on which each thing was created. They may write the answers as you read, if they cannot remember them until you have finished.

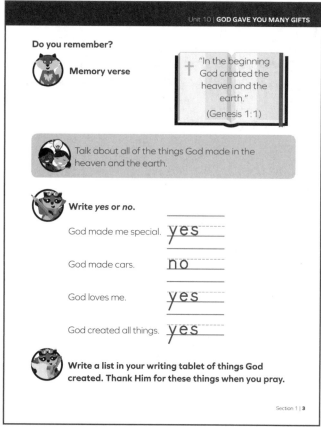

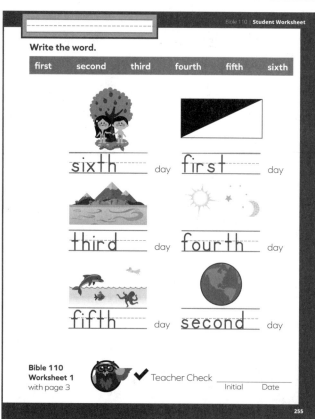

Reread if necessary.

Check together and discuss with the appropriate verse.

Let the children color the pictures.

PAGE 4: GOD LOVES HIS CHILDREN

MATERIALS NEEDED

- Bible
- Bible 102

Concept:

God loves His children.

Objectives:

I can tell how to show my love for God.

I can tell about God's love.

Teacher Goal:

To review concepts taught in Bible 102.

Bible Reference:

2 Corinthians 9:7

Reading Integration:

Main idea, recalling details

Vocabulary:

(Joash, Shadrach, Meshach, Abednego, listens, teaches, gives, heart, praise, trust)
Note: Vocabulary words in parentheses were previously introduced and are being reviewed.

GOD GAVE YOU MANY GIFTS | Unit 10

God Loves His Children

God loves all of His children. He loved Joash, Queen Esther, and Shadrach, Meshach, and Abednego, long ago.

God is our Father. He listens to us. He teaches us. He gives to us.

I am God's child if I ask Jesus into my heart. I praise God. I trust Him.

| Queen Esther

| Joash

| Shadrach, Meshach, & Abednego

4 | Section 1

Teaching Page 4:

Review the stories of Joash, Queen Esther, Shadrach, Meshach, and Abednego from Bible 102.

Have the children read the page silently.

Ask these questions:

"Does God love all His children?"

"Who is our Father?"

"What does He do for us? (listens, teaches, gives)

"Whose child are you if you ask Jesus into your heart?"

Have the page read aloud.

PAGE 5: ACTIVITY PAGE

MATERIALS NEEDED

- pencils
- writing tablet
- Bible
- Bible 102

Teaching Page 5:

Read the memory verse. Help the children find it in the Bible. Review as much as is necessary for your class.

Have the children discuss giving in small groups.

Have them go through Bible 102 as they discuss.

Read the first direction. Let the children complete the activity. Check together and discuss the meaning of each sentence. Read the final direction. Limit the list to one full page. Discuss the lists.

Activities:

1. Review worksheets, projects, and activities for Bible 102 and the "Show Your Love" box (Bible 104).

2. Continue the class prayer booklet. Have the class compare a prayer asking God's help. Write it on chart paper. Have the children decorate the page with illustrations. Add to prayer chart made for page 3.

PAGE 6: GOD WANTS YOU TO DO GOOD

MATERIALS NEEDED

- Bible
- pencils
- writing tablet

Concept:

God wants you to do good.

Objective:

I can tell how to show my love for God.

Teacher Goal:

To review the concepts taught in Bible 104.

Bible Reference:

Matthew 22:39

Reading Integration:

Main idea, recalling details, speaking in a group

Vocabulary:

(yourself, show, helping, sharing, obeying, truth)

Note: Vocabulary words in parentheses were previously introduced and are being reviewed.

GOD GAVE YOU MANY GIFTS | Unit 10

God Wants You to Do Good

Jesus told you
that you should love God,
love others, and love yourself.
You show your love for God
by doing good.

You show your love for others
by helping, by obeying, by sharing,
by praying and by _____ .

You show your love for yourself
by being kind, by telling the truth,
by obeying, and by _____ .

6 | Section 1

Teaching Page 6:

Have a volunteer read the title. Ask how the children in the picture are being good.

Read the first paragraph. Have the children recall the two great commandments.

Read the second paragraph.

Ask volunteers to finish the two sentences. Discuss ways in which they can help, obey, share, pray, and so on.

Activity:

Have the children write other ways of showing love for themselves and for others in their writing tablets. Allow time to share these ways in small groups or with the whole class.

PAGE 7: ACTIVITY PAGE

MATERIALS NEEDED

- pencils
- writing tablet
- Bible 104
- Worksheet 2

Teaching Page 7:

Review the memory verse.

Let the children complete the discussion activity in groups of three or four. Have them go over Bible 104 as part of the discussion.

Read the first direction. Let them complete the activity independently. Check together and have the children tell how to change the *no* statement to a *yes* statement.

Read the final direction. Limit the list to no more than one full page. Allow time to share the lists. At the end of this time, stop for a moment of silent prayer. Tell the children to ask God to help them be kind.

Activities:

1. Review worksheets, activities, and projects from Bible 104.

2. Do Worksheet 2.

   Read the direction. Let the children complete the Worksheet.

   Check by having the children tell why they did or did not circle the picture.

   Have them write one sentence for each picture in their writing tablets.

   Let them color the pictures when their work is finished.

3. Have the children do a class project that will help someone in the school or community (write notes to a sick person, send welcome cards to a new family, send thank-you notes to school or church helpers, collect toys for a poor family, etc.).

The students should prepare for the Self Test. Ask the students to look over and read the Self Test but they should not write the answers to any questions. After looking over the Self Test the students should go to the beginning of the unit and reread the text and review the answers to the activities up to the Self Test.

The students are to complete the Self Test the next school day. This should be done under regular test conditions without allowing the students to look back. A good idea is to clip the pages together before the test.

PAGE 8: SELF TEST 1

MATERIALS NEEDED

• pencils

Concept:

Evaluation.

Objectives:

I can tell about God's creation.

I can tell how to show my love for God.

Teacher Goal:

To check each child's progress.

Bible References:

Review all references.

Reading Integration:

Following directions, recalling details

Vocabulary:

Review all vocabulary words.

Teaching Page 8:

Read all of the directions at least once. Have the children repeat what they must do.

Any two of the three memory verses in Section 1 are acceptable. More advanced children may be expected to recite all three verses.

Check immediately. Review any concepts missed or have an aide work with individuals who have not done well.

2.   GOD'S WORD

PAGE 9

MATERIALS NEEDED

• Bible

Concept:

The Bible is God's Word.

Objective:

I can tell about God's Word.

Teacher Goals:

To review God's Word and to recall missionaries and their work.

Reading Integration:

Main idea

Vocabulary:

(Old Testament, New Testament, missionaries)
Note: Vocabulary words in parentheses were previously introduced and are being reviewed.

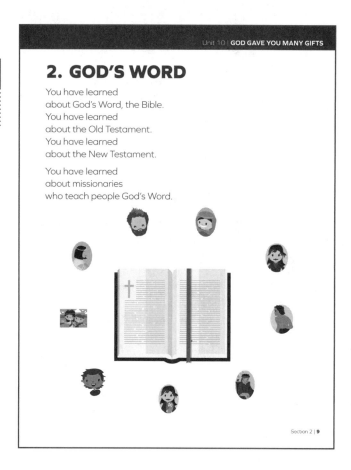

Unit 10 | **GOD GAVE YOU MANY GIFTS**

2. GOD'S WORD

You have learned
about God's Word, the Bible.
You have learned
about the Old Testament.
You have learned
about the New Testament.

You have learned
about missionaries
who teach people God's Word.

Section 2 | **9**

Teaching Page 9:

Have the children open their Bibles and show you the two parts that make up the Bible.

Read page 9 to the children or have it read.

Discuss the illustrations. See how many the children can recall from Bible 105 and 109.

Ask the children what they recall about missionaries (Bible 108). Ask them if they remember how they can be missionaries.

PAGES 10 AND 11: THE OLD TESTAMENT IS GOD'S WORD

MATERIALS NEEDED

- Bible
- Bible 105

Concept:

The Old Testament is God's Word.

Objective:

I can tell about God's Word.

Teacher Goal:

To review the concepts and stories taught in Bible 105.

Bible References:

All Bible stories from Bible 105.

Reading Integration:

Main idea, recalling details

Vocabulary:

(Joseph, Elijah, Jonathan, David, Miriam, Deborah, Ishmael, Mephibosheth)
Note: Vocabulary words in parentheses were previously introduced and are being reviewed.

Teaching Pages 10 and 11:

Identify each picture on page 10 and ask the children what they remember about each one. Have them find each one's name again on the page (paragraph 2).

Read the page to the children pausing in paragraph two so that the children connect the name with the pictures.

Have the children tell one thing about each person in response to the question.

Read the first paragraph on page 11. Ask the children to answer the question. If they cannot remember, tell them to find the story in Bible 105 and read the answer.

Follow the same procedure for paragraphs two and three.

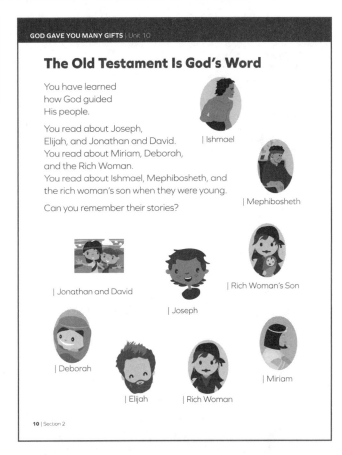

PAGES 12 AND 13: ACTIVITY PAGES

MATERIALS NEEDED

- pencils
- writing tablet
- Worksheet 3

Teaching Pages 12 and 13:

Read the paragraph at the top of page 12.

Have the children discuss the question in small groups using Section 2 of Bible 105 as a guide.

Read the direction sentence. Review the three names. Have the children write the names under the pictures. Check by having the children retell the story as they name the picture.

Review the memory verse as needed.

Have the children discuss these questions as a class. Make a list of their suggestions on the board.

Let them do the matching exercise independently. Check together.

Activities:

1. Review stories, worksheets, projects, and activities from Bible 105. Complete any activities not done when the LIFEPAC was first covered.

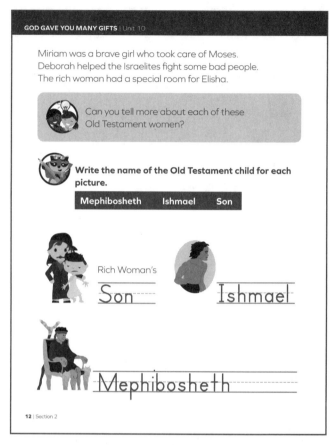

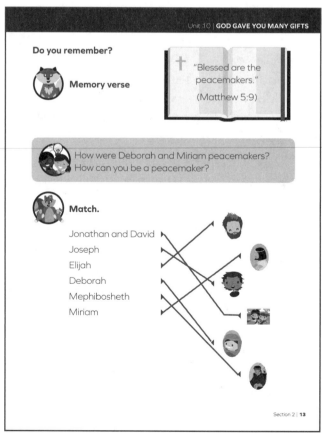

2. Do Worksheet 3.

   This Worksheet reviews the story of young Moses. Have the children draw their picture and write one paragraph about the story in their writing tablets. Check by having the paragraph read when the picture is shown.

PAGE 14: THE NEW TESTAMENT IS GOD'S WORD

MATERIALS NEEDED

- Bible
- Bible 109

Concept:

The New Testament is God's Word.

Objective:

I can tell about God's Word.

Teacher Goal:

To review the concepts taught in Bible 109.

Bible References:

Review all Bible stories from Bible 109.

Reading Integration:

Main idea, recalling details

Vocabulary:

(Lazarus, Thomas, Stephen, Mary, Anna, Lydia)
Note: Vocabulary words in parentheses were previously introduced and are being reviewed.

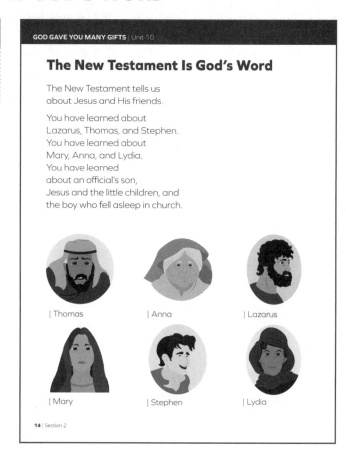

GOD GAVE YOU MANY GIFTS | Unit 10

The New Testament Is God's Word

The New Testament tells us about Jesus and His friends.

You have learned about Lazarus, Thomas, and Stephen. You have learned about Mary, Anna, and Lydia. You have learned about an official's son, Jesus and the little children, and the boy who fell asleep in church.

| Thomas | Anna | Lazarus

| Mary | Stephen | Lydia

14 | Section 2

Teaching Page 14:

Identify all the illustrations. Have the children find the names again on the page. Ask which people from Bible 109 are not illustrated (the children).

Read the page to the children. Pause while they identify the pictures as the names are read.

PAGE 15: ACTIVITY PAGE

MATERIALS NEEDED

- pencils
- writing tablet

Teaching Page 15:

Read the directions. Divide the class into four groups. Assign one picture to each group. Have the children talk about their story, retell it, and prepare to act it out for the class.

When they are ready, let each group take their turn acting out the story. Encourage them to speak clearly.

Have the children write one paragraph in their writing tablets about the story they like best. Collect and correct. Return and have the children correct the mistakes, recopy their stories, and take their paragraphs home.

PAGE 16: ACTIVITY PAGE

MATERIALS NEEDED

- Bible
- Bible 109

Teaching Page 16:

This page reviews three stories from Bible 109.

Read the first paragraph or have it read. Give several children an opportunity to answer. If they cannot remember, have them find the story in Bible 109 and reread it.

Follow the same procedure for the final two paragraphs.

Activities:

1. Complete or review activities and worksheets for these stories from Bible 109.

2. Have the children make a story booklet for one of the three stories on this page.

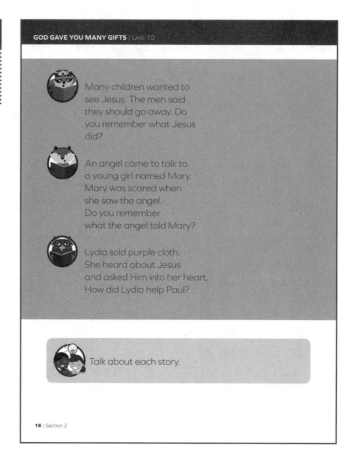

PAGE 17: ACTIVITY PAGE

MATERIALS NEEDED

- pencils
- writing tablet
- Worksheet 4

Teaching Page 17:

Read the memory verse. This verse will take more review because of its length and the difficulty of some words. Remind them what the verse means.

Read the first direction. Give help with the vocabulary as needed. When they have finished, have the children read and discuss each answer. Have them change the two *no* statements to *yes* statements.

Read the final direction. When they have finished the activity, let them share their sentences in small groups.

Activities:

1. Review Bible 109 and any materials in the teacher's guide that will help the children with the review.

2. Do Worksheet 4.

   This worksheet provides further review of the New Testament stories and checks the children's ability to put things in order.

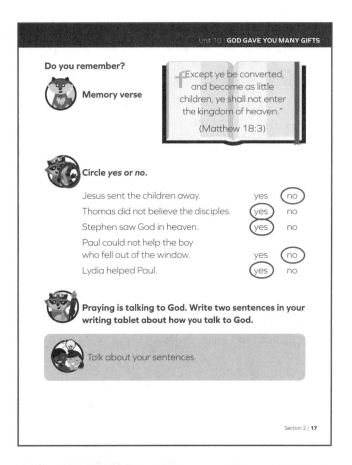

PAGE 18: MISSIONARIES SPREAD GOD'S WORD

MATERIALS NEEDED

- pencils
- writing tablet
- Bible
- Bible 108

Concept:

Missionaries spread God's Word.

Objective:

I can tell about God's Word.

Teacher Goal:

To review the concepts taught in Bible 108.

Bible References:

James 1:22, Bible stories from Bible 108, Section 1

Reading Integration:

Main idea

Vocabulary:

(missionaries, pastors, doctors, translators, radio, neighborhood)
Note: Vocabulary words in parentheses were previously introduced and are being reviewed.

Teaching Page 18:

Review the stories of Stephen, Paul, and the woman at the well from Bible 108. Discuss the illustrations. Have the children recall the types of missionaries talked about in Bible 108.

Read the page to the children. Recall work missionaries do and the ways in which the children can be missionaries.

Activities:

1. Have the children select one type of missionary they have studied. Have them write two paragraphs about the type missionary they have chosen. Have them illustrate their paragraphs. Make a bulletin board display on missionaries with the pictures and stories.

2. Have the children make a booklet showing the ways in which they can be missionaries.

3. Select a missionary project for the class. Have them help someone in the neighborhood, write to missionaries abroad, and so on.

PAGE 19: ACTIVITY PAGE

MATERIALS NEEDED

• pencils
• writing tablet

Teaching Page 19:

Review the memory verse and continue the discussion of how the children can be missionaries.

Read the first direction. Read the sentences as well if the children need help. Check together and discuss.

Read the final direction. When the children finish their sentences, have them share with the group.

The students should prepare for the Self Test. Ask the students to look over and read the Self Test but they should not write the answers to any questions. After looking over the Self Test the students should go to the beginning of the unit and reread the text and review the answers to the activities up to the Self Test.

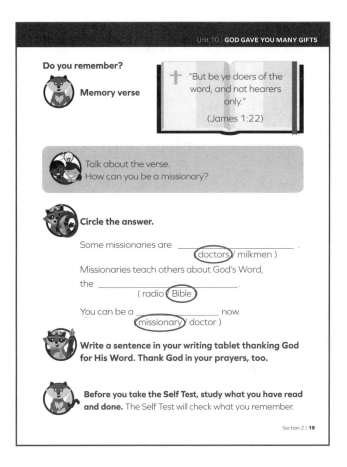

The students are to complete the Self Test the next school day. This should be done under regular test conditions without allowing the students to look back. A good idea is to clip the pages together before the test.

PAGE 20: SELF TEST 2

MATERIALS NEEDED

• pencils

Concept:

Evaluation.

Objectives:

I can tell about God's Creation.

I can tell how to show my love for God.

I can tell about God's Word.

Bible References:

Review all memory verses and stories.

Reading Integration:

Following directions, recalling details

Vocabulary:

Review all vocabulary words.

Teaching Page 20:

Read all the directions and the sentences if necessary.

Let the children complete the written part of the test independently.

Let them recite any four of the six memory verses in Sections 1 and 2. Make allowances for students who cannot memorize easily.

Check immediately and review any areas in which the children still need review.

Activity:

Put the names of all the Old and New Testament people studied in a large box. Have several children draw a name from the box. Let each in turn tell the story for the name they have picked. If they cannot tell the story, they lose their turn and the name is put back in the box. The game ends when all the slips have been gone through. The child or children who have completed the most stories win the game.

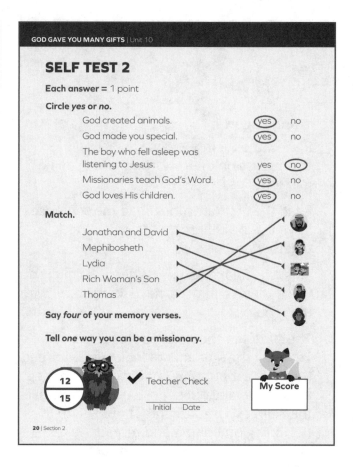

3.   GOD'S SON

PAGE 21

MATERIALS NEEDED

• Bible 106 and 107

Concept:

Jesus is God's Son.

Objective:

I can tell what Jesus did.

Teacher Goal:

To remind the children of God's greatest gift.

Reading Integration:

Main idea, recalling details

Vocabulary:

(Savior, promised)
Note: Vocabulary words in parentheses were previously introduced and are being reviewed.

Unit 10 | **GOD GAVE YOU MANY GIFTS**

3. GOD'S SON

The best gift God gave us was His Son.

You have learned that Adam and Eve disobeyed God.

You learned that God promised to send a Savior. That Savior was His only Son, Jesus Christ.

Section 3 | **21**

Teaching Page 21:

Tell the children that in Section 3 they will review what they have learned about the life of Jesus.

Discuss the illustrations. Have the children try to recall the stories for each.

Have the children read the page silently.

Ask these questions:

"What was God's best gift?"

"What did Adam and Eve do?"

"What was God's promise?"

"Who was Jesus Christ?"

Reread the page aloud with the children to make sure they have understood all of it.

PAGE 22: JESUS CAME

MATERIALS NEEDED

- Bible
- Bible 106
- map of Holy Land

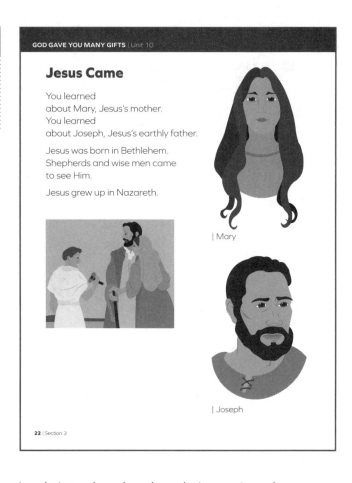

GOD GAVE YOU MANY GIFTS | Unit 10

Jesus Came

You learned
about Mary, Jesus's mother.
You learned
about Joseph, Jesus's earthly father.

Jesus was born in Bethlehem.
Shepherds and wise men came
to see Him.

Jesus grew up in Nazareth.

| Mary

| Joseph

22 | Section 3

Concept:

Jesus was born in Bethlehem and lived in Nazareth.

Objective:

I can tell what Jesus did.

Teacher Goal:

To review the concepts taught in Bible 106.

Bible References:

Luke chapters 1 and 2

Reading Integration:

Main idea, listening, recalling details

Vocabulary:

(stepfather, Bethlehem, Nazareth, shepherds)
Note: Vocabulary words in parentheses were previously introduced and are being reviewed.

Teaching Page 22:

Use the illustrations to have the children recall parts of the story of Jesus's childhood.

Have two children read the page. Ask the class to fill in the missing details. Use the map to remind the children of the locations they have learned about in Bible 106.

Activities:

1. Review maps, worksheets, activities, booklets, and so on from Bible 106.

2. Divide the class into four groups. Assign each group a part of Jesus's early life (birthday, visit of Wise Men, flight into Egypt, growing up in Nazareth, visits to the Temple, etc.). Let an aide work with the group. Have the children discuss the story assigned to them and then prepare to act out that story. Allow time for each group to present their play to the entire class.

PAGE 23: ACTIVITY PAGE

MATERIALS NEEDED

- pencils
- writing tablet
- Worksheet 5

Teaching Page 23:

Read the memory verse with the children. Remind them what the words *increased*, *wisdom*, *stature*, and *favor* mean.

Have the children discuss the verse. If they have forgotten the story, reread it from Luke or have the children find and read it in Bible 106.

Read the first direction. Have the children read the two words and then complete the two sentences. Check together and have the children find each city on the map.

Read the final direction. Have the children tell you what they are to do. Limit the list to one full page at most. Share the lists when they have finished. Have the children bow their heads and ask God's help silently.

Activities:

1. Add a prayer for wisdom to the class prayer booklet. Have the children compose the prayer. Write it down on chart paper. Have the children decorate the border. Add the chart to the other prayer charts and use the prayer before study time.

2. Do Worksheet 5.

   Read the direction to the children. Remind them to trace the path with their finger before using a pencil. Review the story.

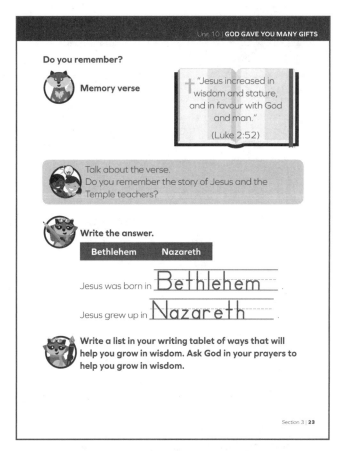

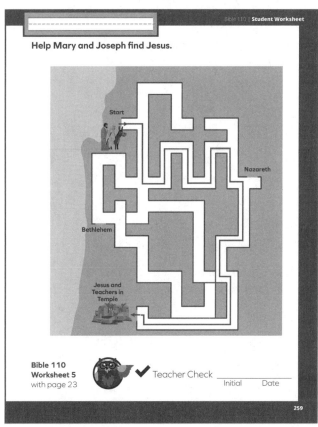

PAGE 24: JESUS TAUGHT

MATERIALS NEEDED

- Bible
- Bible 107

Concept:

Jesus taught in many ways.

Objective:

I can tell what Jesus did.

Teacher Goal:

To review the concepts taught in Bible 107, Sections 1 and 2.

Bible References:

Bible stories used in Bible 107

Reading Integration:

Main idea, listening, recalling details

Vocabulary:

(Gospels, taught)
Note: Vocabulary words in parentheses were previously introduced and are being reviewed.

GOD GAVE YOU MANY GIFTS | Unit 10

Jesus Taught

Jesus taught you how to live.
His life is told
in the Gospels.
Jesus taught by talking to people.
Jesus taught
by telling special stories.
Jesus taught
by doing special things.

Can you remember
some of the special things
Jesus said and did?

24 | Section 3

Teaching Page 24:

Have a child read the title. Ask the children if they remember how Jesus taught and what he used to teach.

Read the first paragraph.

Ask these questions:

"How many Gospels are there?"

"Do you remember who wrote the Gospels ?"

"Do you remember what the special stories Jesus told are called?"

"Do you remember what the special things Jesus did are called?"

"What special thing does the picture show?" (Jesus calming sea and wind)

Read the final paragraph.

Ask the children to tell about other things they have learned about Jesus's teaching (Sermon on the Mount, giving sight to blind man, raising Jairus' daughter, etc.).

Activities:

1. Review booklets, worksheets, and so on for Bible 107.

2. Have the children act out or retell the stories of some of the parables and miracles with puppets or stick figures.

PAGE 25: ACTIVITY PAGE

MATERIALS NEEDED

• Bible
• Bible 107

Teaching Page 25:

Divide the children into four groups.

Appoint a leader for each group.

Assign one of the stories to each group. Have the group discuss the story as they retell it. Have the children prepare a reading of the story from Bible 107 or from a children's Bible.

When they are ready, allow time for each group to present its reading to the class. Have the whole class discuss each story after it is presented.

Unit 10 | **GOD GAVE YOU MANY GIFTS**

Talk about the story for each picture.

Section 3 | **25**

PAGE 26: THE LORD'S PRAYER

MATERIALS NEEDED

- Bible
- Bible 103

Concept:

The Lord's Prayer.

Objectives:

I can tell what Jesus did.

I can tell how to pray.

Teacher Goal:

To review the Lord's Prayer.

Bible Reference:

Matthew 6:9–13

Reading Integration:

Main idea, speaking in a group

Vocabulary:

(disciples)
Note: Vocabulary words in parentheses were previously introduced and are being reviewed.

GOD GAVE YOU MANY GIFTS | Unit 10

One thing that Jesus taught was a very special prayer.

He taught the disciples the Lord's Prayer.

Can you say the Lord's Prayer?

Say and talk about the Lord's Prayer.

26 | Section 3

Teaching Page 26:

Discuss the illustration and the sermon on the Mount. Discuss the things they have learned about that special sermon (review all parts covered in Bible 107, 104, and 103).

Have the children read the page silently.

Ask these questions:

"What did Jesus teach His disciples?"

"Do you remember the Lord's Prayer?"

"Can you say the Lord's Prayer?"

Have the children talk about the Lord's Prayer as they say it. Discuss each verse.

PAGE 27: ACTIVITY PAGE

MATERIALS NEEDED

• pencils
• writing tablet
• Bible 107

Teaching Page 27:

Read the memory verse phrase by phrase. Read it several times and have the children repeat it. Send copies of the verse home for review.

Discuss the verse in relation to the three stories studied in Bible 107 (Mark 2:3–12; John 9; Mark 7:32–37).

Read both directions. Have the children repeat what they are to do. When they have finished, check by having the children read their sentences as they tell the correct sequence for the story. Review the story (Mark 4:36–41).

Activities:

1. Have the children choose one of the three healing stories. Have them write about the story (about three paragraphs). Check the stories and have them recopy them and paste them on large drawing paper. Have them illustrate the story. When they have finished, make a display of the stories, have the children take them home, or have them give the stories to someone who does not know the wonderful things Jesus has done.

2. Do special practice drills on the memory verse with the slower students. Do the verse as a choral reading, having the children act out parts of the verse, or have the children say it in turns, each taking a part.

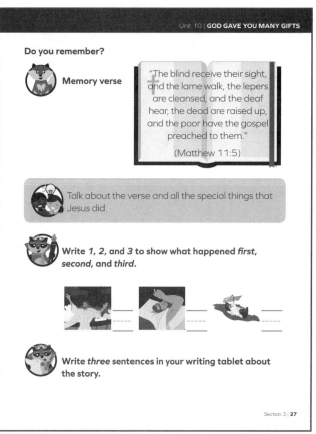

PAGES 28 AND 29: JESUS DIED FOR US

MATERIALS NEEDED

- Bible
- Bible 107

Concept:

Jesus died to save us.

Objective:

I can tell what Jesus did.

Teacher Goal:

To review the concepts taught in Bible 107, Section 3.

Bible References:

Gospel accounts of the passion and death of Christ

Reading Integration:

Main idea, recalling details, speaking in a group

Vocabulary:

(Jerusalem)

Note: Vocabulary words in parentheses were previously introduced and are being reviewed.

Teaching Pages 28 and 29:

Have the children read both pages silently.

Ask these questions:

"Why did God send Jesus?"

"What did Jesus have to do to save us?"

"Where did He go?"

"What did some men do to Him?"

"Where did Jesus die?"

"Who is saved?"

"What does the picture on page 28 show?"

"What does the picture on page 29 show?"

Read both pages aloud. Clarify any points that are not clear. If the children have forgotten anything, have them review Bible 107 or read the text from the Gospel.

GOD GAVE YOU MANY GIFTS | Unit 10

Jesus Can Save Us

God sent Jesus
to save all of us
from sin.

You learned
that Jesus had to die.

He went up to Jerusalem.
He was taken by some men.
They wanted Him to die.

28 | Section 3

Unit 10 | **GOD GAVE YOU MANY GIFTS**

Some men took Jesus
out of the city.
They nailed Him
to the cross.

Jesus died on the cross.
He died to save us.
All people who ask Jesus
into their lives are saved.

Section 3 | **29**

PAGES 30 AND 31: RESURRECTION AND ASCENSION

MATERIALS NEEDED

- Bible
- Bible 107
- crayons
- scissors
- Worksheet 6

Concept:

Jesus rose and returned to His Father.

Objective:

I can tell what Jesus did.

Teacher Goal:

To review the Resurrection and Ascension.

Bible References:

Gospel accounts of the Resurrection and Ascension

Reading Integration:

Main idea, recalling details, speaking in a group

Vocabulary:

(Resurrection, heaven)
Note: Vocabulary words in parentheses were previously introduced and are being reviewed.

Teaching Pages 30 and 31:

Have the children read both pages silently.

Ask these questions:

"What happened on the third day after Jesus died?"

"What did Jesus tell His friends?"

"What is happening in the picture on page 30?"

"What is happening in the picture on page 31?"

Read the pages aloud.

Talk about the importance of Jesus's death and Resurrection for all for us.

GOD GAVE YOU MANY GIFTS | Unit 10

On the third day
after He died,
Jesus came back to life.
Jesus saw His friends.
They were very happy.

Talk about Jesus's death and Resurrection.

30 | Section 3

Unit 10 | **GOD GAVE YOU MANY GIFTS**

Jesus told His friends
that the time had come
to return to His Father
in heaven.

Section 3 | **31**

Activities

1. Do Worksheet 6.

   Have the children read the banner. Explain what the word *Alleluia* means. Have the children color the banner, cut it out, and hang it somewhere where it will remind them of all that Jesus did for them.

2. Read the Gospel account of the things Jesus did between His Resurrection and Ascension. Review His message to go and teach all nations (Matthew 28:19).

PAGE 32: ACTIVITY PAGE

MATERIALS NEEDED

• pencils
• writing tablet

Teaching Page 32:

Review the memory verse.

Read the first direction. Have the children do the activity independently. Check together and discuss each sentence as a review.

Read the final direction. Make sure the children know what they are to do. Have the children write their sentences and pray quietly.

The students should prepare for the Self Test. Ask the students to look over and read the Self Test but they should not write the answers to any questions. After looking over the Self Test the students should go to the beginning of the unit and reread the text and review the answers to the activities up to the Self Test.

The students are to complete the Self Test the next school day. This should be done under regular test conditions without allowing the students to look back. A good idea is to clip the pages together before the test.

PAGE 33: SELF TEST 3

MATERIALS NEEDED

• pencils

Concept:

Evaluation.

Objectives:

I can tell about God's Creation.

I can tell how to show my love for God.

I can tell about God's Word.

I can tell what Jesus did.

I can tell how to pray.

I can tell about God's love.

Teacher Goal:

To check each child's progress.

Bible References:

Review all memory verses.

Reading Integration:

Recalling details, following directions

Vocabulary:

Review all vocabulary words.

Teaching Page 33:

Read all the directions. Let the children complete the written activities independently. Have an aide or parent help with the oral section.

The child may recite any five of the nine verses from the LIFEPAC. Do not require that number of the slower students.

Check immediately. Review any concepts missed before going on to the LIFEPAC Test.

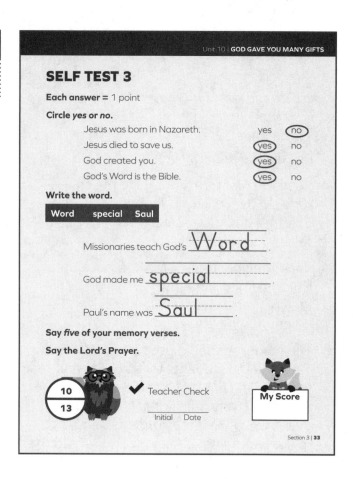

LIFEPAC TEST 110

Administer the test to the class as a group. Ask to have directions read or read them to the class. In either case, be sure that the children clearly understand. Put examples on the board if it seems necessary. Give ample time for each activity to be completed before going to the next.

Correct immediately and discuss with the child.

Review any concepts that have been missed.

Give those children who do not achieve the 80% score additional copies of the worksheets and a list of vocabulary words to study. A parent or a classroom helper should help in the review.

When the child is ready, give the Alternate LIFEPAC Test. Use the same procedure as for the LIFEPAC Test.

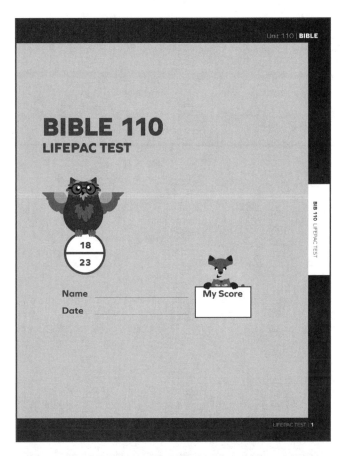

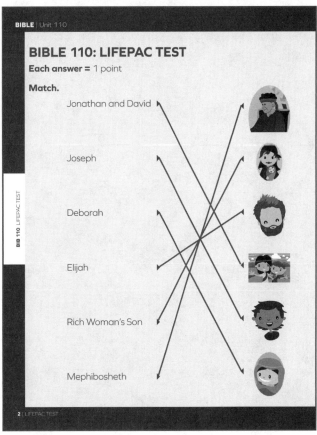

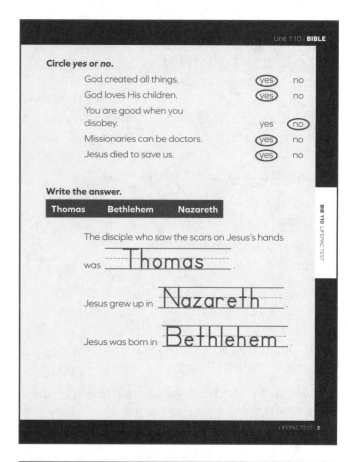

Circle *yes* or *no*.

God created all things.	(yes)	no
God loves His children.	(yes)	no
You are good when you disobey.	yes	(no)
Missionaries can be doctors.	(yes)	no
Jesus died to save us.	(yes)	no

Write the answer.

Thomas	Bethlehem	Nazareth

The disciple who saw the scars on Jesus's hands was ___Thomas___.

Jesus grew up in ___Nazareth___.

Jesus was born in ___Bethlehem___.

BIB 110 LIFEPAC TEST

LIFEPAC TEST | 3

Write *1*, *2*, and *3* to show what happened *first*, *second*, and *third*.

___2___

___1___

___3___

Say *five* memory verses.

Say "the Lord's Prayer."

BIB 110 LIFEPAC TEST

ALTERNATE LIFEPAC TEST 110

Administer the test to the class as a group. Ask to have directions read or read them to the class. In either case, be sure that the children clearly understand. Put examples on the board if it seems necessary. Give ample time for each activity to be completed before going to the next.

Correct immediately and discuss with the child.

Review any concepts that have been missed.

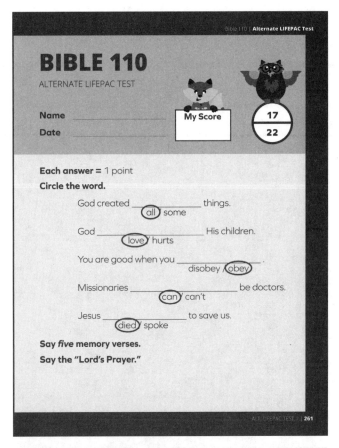

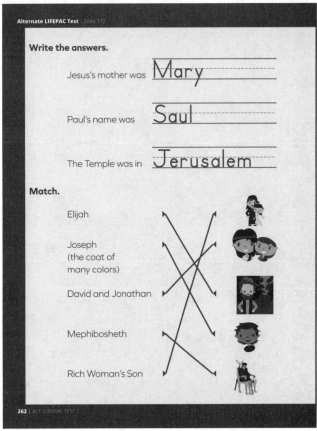

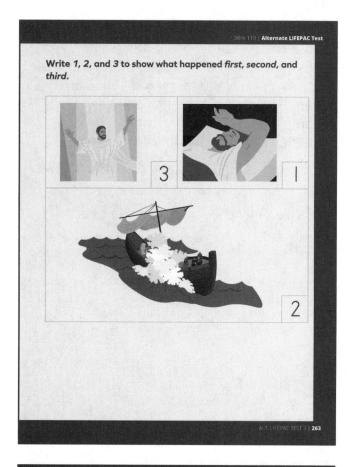

_____

Write the word.

| first | second | third | fourth | fifth | sixth |

_____
- -
_____ day

_____
- -
_____ day

_____
- -
_____ day

_____
- -
_____ day

_____
- -
_____ day

_____
- -
_____ day

**Bible 110
Worksheet 1**
with page 3

✔ Teacher Check _____

Initial   Date

Circle the children who show their love.

Bible 110
Worksheet 2
with page 7

✔ Teacher Check _____

Initial   Date

Draw what happened next.

Bible 110
Worksheet 3
with page 13

Teacher Check _____

Initial   Date

Write *1*, *2*, and *3* to show what happened *first*, *second*, and *third*.

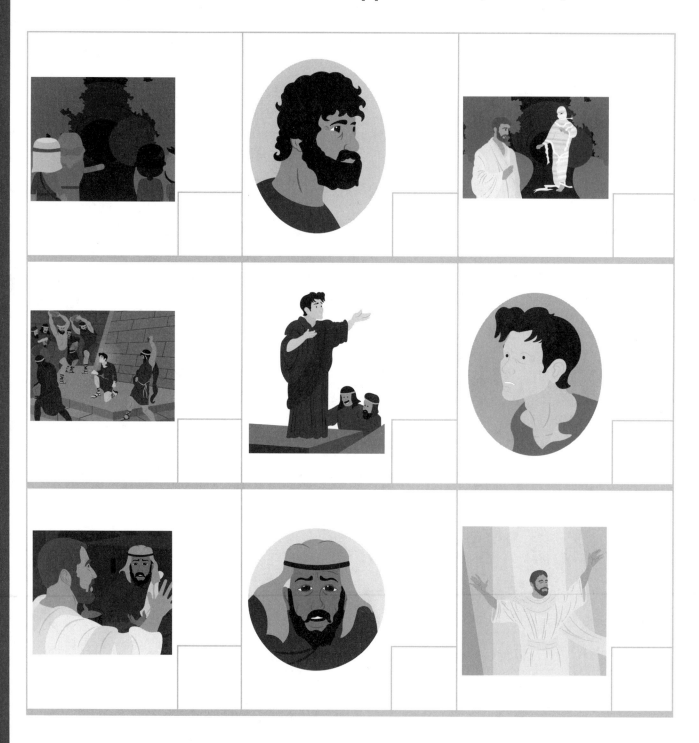

Bible 110
Worksheet 4
with page 17

Teacher Check _____
                        Initial   Date

Help Mary and Joseph find Jesus.

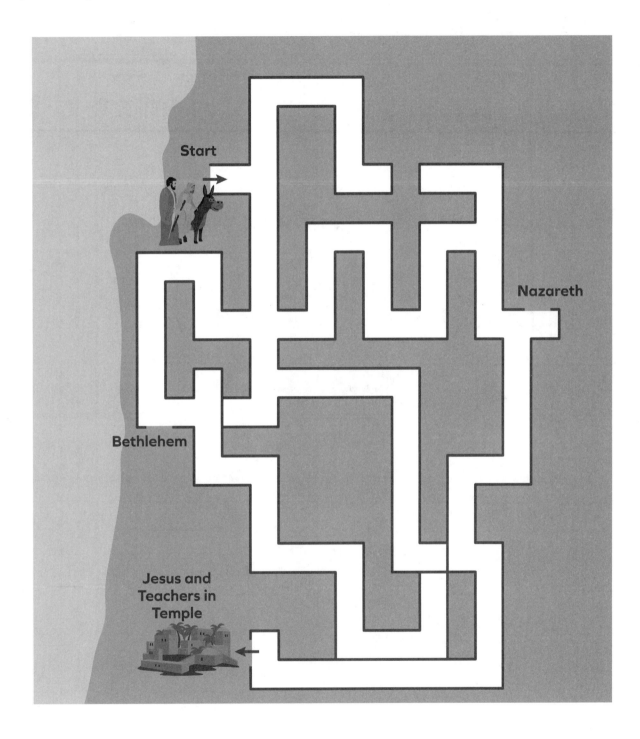

Start

Nazareth

Bethlehem

Jesus and
Teachers in
Temple

Teacher Check _____
Initial   Date

He is Risen! Alleluia!

**Bible 110
Worksheet 6**
with page 31

✔ Teacher Check _____

Initial   Date

BIBLE 110

ALTERNATE LIFEPAC TEST

Name _____

Date _____

My Score

17
22

Each answer = 1 point

Circle the word.

God created _____ things.
all / some

God _____ His children.
love / hurts

You are good when you _____ .
disobey / obey

Missionaries _____ be doctors.
can / can't

Jesus _____ to save us.
died / spoke

Say *five* memory verses.

Say the "Lord's Prayer."

Write the answers.

Jesus's mother was _____

Paul's name was _____

The Temple was in _____

Match.

Elijah ▶ ◀

Joseph
(the coat of
many colors) ▶ ◀

David and Jonathan ▶ ◀

Mephibosheth ▶ ◀

Rich Woman's Son ▶ ◀

Write *1, 2,* and *3* to show what happened *first, second,* and *third.*

CUMULATIVE WORD LIST

Abigail	button	didn't	funny	Jacob
Abraham	care	died	Gabriel	Jairus
Adam	cats	different	gate	jealous
afraid	chains	direct	gave	Jericho
alike	chart	disciples	giant	Jesus
allowed	cheerfully	dogs	gifts	John
altar	child	done	give	Jonah
always	children	Dorcas	glorify	Jordan River
amid	Christ	down	glory	Joseph
angel	Christians	draw	God	Joshua
animals	church	earth	Goliath	journey
Anna	cities	eat	good	Julie
answer	city	Elisha	Gospel	kind
anyone	classmates	else	grain	kingdom
anytime	clothes	enemies	grass	knew
anywhere	coal	especially	great	lad
arise	coat	Esther	green	laid
army	collector	Eve	guards	lakes
asking	copied	everything	guided	lame
baby	coughed	evil	hallowed	land
balloon	could	faces	happened	language
basket	countries	family	haste	laughed
beautiful	crayons	farmer	healed	law
before	create	Father	hear	lead
believed	creatures	favorite	hearts	leader
Bethlehem	crippled	fearfully	heaven	learn
better	Cross	fed	helper	lesson
Bible	crowd	feed	Herod	letter
birds	daily	felt	hole	lie
blessed	Daniel	fight	horns	light
blind	daughter	fish(es)	houses	lions
blinded	David	flat	however	litter
Boaz	days	flew	hungry	little
book	daytime	flower(s)	hurt	loaves
box	deaf	flying	hurting	Luke
brave	debts	food	husband	made
bread	decided	forever	idea	maid
bright	deeds	forgive	important	many
brothers	deep	forgiveness	Isaac	Mark
busy	deliver	found	Isaiah	market
butterflies	delivered	friends	Israel	married

Martha	Paul	seven	Temple	women
martyr	peacemaker	sew	temptation	wonderfully
Mary	people	shalt	test	word
master	person	share	thanked	work
Matthew	Peter	sheep	thank you	world
mean	pets	shepherds	thee	worry
medical	place	shine	themselves	yourself
memory verse	plan	ship	therefore	Zacchaeus
Messiah	plants	short	things	Zacharias
Micah	play	shout	thinks	
minute	please	show	third	
miracle	power	sick	thou	
missionaries	praise	signal	thought	
missionary	prayer	silly	three	
money	pretty	silver	through	
morning	prices	Simeon	thy	
Moses	prison	sing	thyself	
mother	problem	sister(s)	today	
mountain	promise(s)	sleep	together	
mouths	promised	sling	trace	
much	prophet	slowly	translators	
Naaman	queen	smile	trees	
Nabal	radio	sold	tricked	
Naomi	reaches	someday	trouble	
nations	remember	soul	trust	
Nazareth	respect	sower	trusted	
need	return	special	turns	
needed	right	stable	unscramble	
neighbor(s)	risen	stars	unto	
neighborhood	rivers	start	upon	
never	roof	stepfather	upset	
night	rose	Stephen	voice	
noise	Ruth	still	walls	
obey	sacrifice	stones	wanted	
obeying	said	stories	wash	
oceans	sailors	storm	water	
old	salvation	story	whatever	
once	Saul	Sunday	where	
orders	save	swallow	while	
other	Savior	swim	who	
outside	sea	swung	whole	
owl	second	sycamore	wicked	
parable	sent	talk	wide	
parents	servant	taught	wife	
pastors	serve	teacher	woman	

CUMULATIVE LIST OF MEMORY VERSES

LIFEPAC 101:

101.1 "In the beginning God created the heaven and the earth." Genesis 1:1

101.2 "God created man in His own image." Genesis 1:27

LIFEPAC 102:

102.1 "Casting all your care upon him; for he careth for you." 1 Peter 5:7

102.2 "We love him, because he first loved us." 1 John 4:19

102.3 "If ye love me, keep my commandments." Matthew 28:20

LIFEPAC 103:

103.1 "I have called upon thee, for thou wilt hear me, O God." Psalm 17:6

103.2 "Ask and it shall be given you." Luke 11:9

103.3 "My voice shalt thou hear in the morning, O LORD; in the morning will I direct my prayer unto thee." Psalm 5:3

LIFEPAC 104:

104.1 "Love the LORD thy God with all thy heart and with all thy soul and with all thy mind." Matthew 22:37

104.2 "Love your enemies, ... do good to them that hate you, and pray for them." Matthew 5:44

104.3 "Love thy neighbor as thyself." Matthew 22:39

LIFEPAC 105:

105.1 "And there is a friend that sticketh closer than a brother." Proverbs 18:24

105.2 "The LORD is my strength and song, and he is become my salvation: he is my God." Exodus 15:2a

105.3 "Look not every man on his own things, but every man also on the things of others." Philippians 2:4

LIFEPAC 106:

106.1 "Behold a virgin shall be with child, and shall bring forth a son." Matthew 1:23

106.2 "He shall be great, and shall be called the Son of the Highest." Luke 1:23

106.3 "Jesus increased in wisdom and stature, and in favor with God and man." Luke 2:52

LIFEPAC 107:

107.1 "Let your light shine before men, that they may see your good works, and glorify the Father in heaven." Matthew 5:16

107.2 "The blind receive their sight, and the lame walk, the lepers are cleansed, and the deaf hear, the dead are raised up, and the poor have the gospel preached to them." Matthew 11:5

107.3 "He is risen." Matthew 28:6

LIFEPAC 108:

108.1 "Go ye, into all the world, and preach the gospel to every creature." Mark 16:15

108.2 "Go ye therefore, and teach all nations, baptizing them in the name of the Father, and of the Son and of the Holy Ghost." Matthew 28:19

108.3 "But be ye doers of the word, and not hearers only." James 1:22

108.4 "Let your light so shine before men, that they may see your good works, and glorify your Father which is in heaven." Matthew 5:16

LIFEPAC 109:

109.1 "Blessed are the pure in heart; for they shall see God." Matthew 5:8

109.2 "And she shall bring forth a son, and thou shalt call his name JESUS: for he shall save his people from their sins." Matthew 1:21

109.3 "Suffer the little children to come unto me, and forbid them not: for of such is the kingdom of God." Mark 10:14b

LIFEPAC 110:

110.1 "In the beginning God created the heaven and the earth." Genesis 1:1

110.2 "God loveth a cheerful giver." 2 Corinthians 9:7

110.3 "Love thy neighbor, as thyself." Matthew 22:39

110.4 "Blessed are the peacemakers." Matthew 5:9

110.5 "Except ye be converted, and become as little children, ye shall not enter the kingdom of heaven." Matthew 18:3

110.6 "But be ye doers of the word, and not hearers only." James 1:22

110.7 "Jesus increased in wisdom and stature and in favor with God and man." Luke 2:52

110.8 "The blind receive their sight, and the lame walk the lepers are cleansed, and the deaf hear, the dead are raised up, and the poor have the gospel preached to them." Matthew 11:5

110.9 "He is risen." Matthew 28:6